Insectigations

40 HANDS-ON ACTIVITIES TO EXPLORE THE INSECT WORLD

CINDY BLOBAUM

CHICAGO REVIEW PRESS

NANUET PUBLIC LIBRARY
149 CHURCH STREET
NANUET, NEW YORK 10954
845-623-4281

Library of Congress Cataloging-in-Publication Data

Blobaum, Cindy, 1966–

    Insectigations! : 40 hands-on activities to explore the insect world /
    Cindy Blobaum.— 1st ed.
       p. cm.
    Includes bibliographical references.
    ISBN 1-55652-568-0
    1. Insects—Juvenile literature. 2. Insects—Study and teaching
    (Elementary)—Activity programs. I. Title.
    QL467.2.B59 2005
    595.7—dc22

                               2004028245

Cover design: Sommers Design
Interior illustrations: Gail Rattray
Interior design: Rattray Design

All photographs courtesy of Cindy Blobaum unless otherwise noted.
Butterfly Puddles ©2004 by Highlights for Children, Inc., Columbus, Ohio.

Published by Chicago Review Press, Incorporated
814 North Franklin Street
Chicago, Illinois 60610
ISBN 1-55652-568-0
Printed in the United States of America
5 4 3 2 1

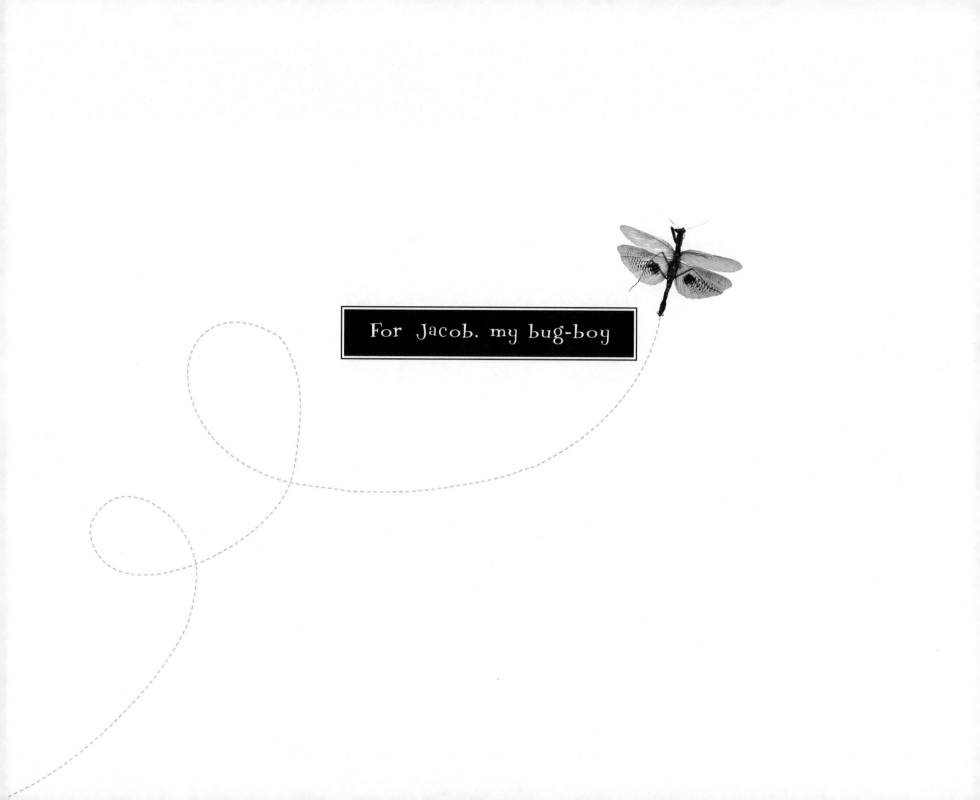

For Jacob, my bug-boy

Contents

Acknowledgments

I unknowingly started research for this book when I became a naturalist and began teaching about insects to thousands of enthusiastic children. Many of my coworkers at the Greenway and Nature Center of Pueblo, Colorado; New Canaan Nature Center in New Canaan, Connecticut; and Neale Woods Nature Center in Omaha, Nebraska, inspired or shared ideas with me that are included in this book. Thank you to all of them.

More recently, Drake University granted me access to its insect collection, Keith Wonder of Hawkeye Fly Fishing Association shared his enthusiasm for and knowledge of fly-fishing, and Robin Pruisner, the State of Iowa Entomologist, provided gypsy moth traps. I appreciate your assistance.

Eli, McKenzie, and Olivia were wonderful models, and thanks to all the 37th Street and Carpenter Avenue families that let me and my children perform final tests of experiments and activities in and around their yards and homes. Thank you to the Blobaum family: Mel, for clipping and mailing all the insect articles you read from magazines and papers; Norman, for your constant interest; Paul, for being my reference resource pinch hitter; Margaret, for the care you have given my kids when I needed it most; and Philip, for understanding what this effort has meant to me. Creating a book is a team effort, and I feel incredibly fortunate to have had the Chicago Review Press team of Cynthia Sherry, Allison Felus, Gerilee Hundt, Brooke Kush, Rattray Design, and Joan Sommers working on my behalf. And I would be remiss if I did not single out Lisa Rosenthal, my insightful and encouraging editor, for a special mention—thank you.

Introduction

On September 9, 1945, Dr. Grace Hopper was putting the Mark II computer at Harvard University through some tests. It had what programmers called a "bug" that was causing it to malfunction. Dr. Hopper pulled out parts, searching for the problem. At 3:45 P.M., she found it. A moth had gotten trapped between points at Relay # 70, Panel F. She removed the moth, carefully taped it into the logbook, and then made a note: "First actual case of (computer) bug being found."

It wasn't really surprising that an insect had found its way into the computer. As long as humans have been around, they have both been bothered by and benefited from insects. Every year, millions of dollars in crops are destroyed by insects. Plagues of locusts have filled the sky and eaten every shred of green plants, causing people to go hungry or migrate to new areas. Fleas were the carriers of black death, a disease that almost wiped out the population of entire cities in Europe in the Middle Ages. Even today, some mosquitoes carry diseases including malaria, which kills millions of people each year.

On the other hand, insects pollinate many of our food plants, including chocolate, apples, and oranges. They help decompose our waste. Ant jaws have been used as stitches in surgery. Fly and beetle larvae help investigators solve crimes. Fruit flies are used in genetic research. People raise insects for food; for their products including silk, honey, and shellac; as pets; and to sell to gardeners, farmers, wedding planners, and educators.

Insects are the largest group of animals in the world, with more than one million different kinds identified and named, and perhaps just as many yet to be discovered. They were around a long time before humans were, and they will help decompose our bodies when we are gone. Since they have been so successful, it makes sense to watch them closely and see what we can learn from them.

In order to observe insects, it helps to have some close at hand. In the following pages you will learn tips and tricks for catching and keeping insects, and how to test the usefulness of an insect exoskeleton, compete against insects in Olympic-style competitions, create a buzzing bug, and train a bee. When you need a live insect for an activity, remember:

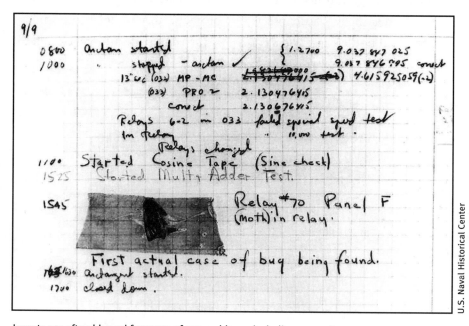

Insects are often blamed for many of our problems, including computer errors.

U.S. Naval Historical Center

they are an important part of our natural ecosystems. Tread lightly through their habitats and collect only the insects you need or can take care of, releasing all the others back where you found them. It is also wise to be like Dr. Hopper and record all your activities in the journal you'll learn how to make in chapter 1. *Journal Notes* at the end of most activities give suggestions for important observations or results to record in your journal.

If you have a strong stomach, make sure you read all the *Gross Entomology* sidebars. You will be amazed at where you can find insects and how they are used. Speaking of finding and using insects, the *Real Entomologists* sidebars tell the true stories of how insects play a part in engineering projects, crime scene investigations, and even food service studies. *Bug Business* sidebars tell about enterprising entomologists who earn money from insects. And you get the shortcuts to finding fun on the Internet in the *Make a Connection* sidebars.

As a special feature, you can test your luck and survival skills as an insect by creating your own *Insectigations!* board game. The materials are easy to find, with instructions for how to make special insect dice in chapter 2, "Body Basics," and details on the game board in chapter 6, "Finders." You use the action cards you create at the end of chapters 2 through 8 to make the path through insect habitats on the game board. The only other things you need are tokens (cicada shells, plastic insects, or decorated bottle caps) and a regular, numbered die. The instructions for putting the game together and the basic rules for playing are at the end of the book.

If you finish trying the experiments and activities and want to do even more, look to the Resources section at the back of the book. There you will discover where to get more information about favorite activities, find connections to entertaining insect festivals, and learn how to participate in ongoing research projects. All you need to do now is turn the page and get going!

1

Getting Started

Ladybug, ladybug, fly away home,

Your house is on fire and your children are alone.

*

You're as busy as a bee.

*

Snug as a bug in a rug.

*

You catch more flies with honey than you do with vinegar.

*

The larger the middle band on a wooly bear caterpillar,
the colder the winter will be.

*

Good night, sleep tight, don't let the bedbugs bite.

From the time you were every young, you have likely heard many sayings like these. What do all these sayings have in common? They show that people have been studying insects for a long time.

The formal name for studying insects is *entomology* (en-ta–MOL-a-jē). Scientists who study insects are called entomologists. What exactly do entomologists do? Some identify and name new insects. Others keep track of insect pests and try to figure out ways to control them. Some try to figure out how to increase the number of insects that help humans. Others try to figure out how insects communicate, how their senses work, or how to use insects to solve human problems. Although humans spend billions of dollars every year on insects, you don't need a lot of money to be a good entomologist. You can find insects wherever you are, and the only equipment you really need is a pencil and a journal.

Make a Journal

Explorers and scientists have long used journals, also called logs, to record what they find, see, hear, and do. Most of the activities in this book include observations or questions for you to answer in your journal. Your notes will become a valuable record of what you see and think, even if you feel your experiences are ordinary or normal. Although any type of notebook will work, the following journal is one you can use for years.

Materials

Three-ring binder with pockets and a clear plastic cover sleeve
Unlined paper
Markers
Lined paper
Hole punch

A three-ring binder makes a great journal for several reasons. It has pockets that can hold pencils, a magnifying lens, ruler, small field guide, and a bandage or two. It is easy to wipe dew, dirt, or mud off the plastic cover. It lies flat when you open it, making it easier to write in. It is simple to add more paper. It is easy to make a new cover and rearrange the contents for science projects or reports.

Use one piece of unlined paper and the markers to create the first cover for your journal. You might want to include your name, a clever title, and some sketches of insects or insect habitats. Slip the cover paper into the clear plastic sleeve.

If your unlined paper doesn't already have holes punched in it, lay a piece of lined paper with holes on top of three sheets of plain paper to use as a guide. Use the hole punch to make three holes so the paper can be put on the rings. Since you should use a separate sheet of paper to record your discoveries for each activity or experiment that you do, repeat this process until you have at least 20 sheets of unlined paper for your journal. Put the unlined paper and at least 20 sheets of lined paper on the rings in your binder. Finally, slip any equipment you want in the pockets, and you are ready to go.

It's essential to include in your journal entries: the date and place of each activity or insect find, the name of the activity (when appropriate), sketches of what you see, and specific things you notice, like how many different colored grasshoppers you find or the sizes of the ants that you catch. Also, copy down the questions from this book so that you know what your answers mean.

Draw an Insect

Even if you are a beginning artist, it is important to include in your journal accurate sketches of the insects you see. You can start by copying other drawings or photographs, but your goal should be to draw from actual insects that you find or catch. Remember, the more you practice, the better your drawings will become.

Materials

Journal
Pencil
Eraser
Insect (or insect picture)

Take a close and careful look at the insect you want to draw. Instead of trying to draw it all at one time, use your imagination to break it down into pieces. Don't worry about the little details at first; just look for shapes you recognize and can draw. It might help to think about traditional

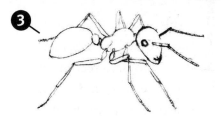

How to shade drawing

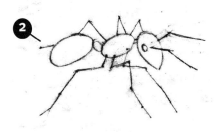

shapes (circle, oval, rectangle, pyramid) or to think about the shapes of common items (egg, crescent moon, ice cream cone, pencil).

Sometimes it is helpful to draw the middle part of the insect first and then think of it as a clock. Where are the legs? At 4:20, 6:30, and 8:40? Where is the head? Where is the abdomen? You also want to think about sizes. It is impossible to make a decent, life-sized drawing of some of the very tiny insects. Instead, for every insect, large or

small, make a line to show its real size, then draw it whatever size you want. What is important is to show relative sizes. Is the head the same size as the body? Half the size? Twice as big? Figure out how big each piece is compared to the others, then lightly sketch the shapes you need together.

When you have drawn all the pieces, erase or adjust any that don't look like you want them to. After you have everything in place, spend some time erasing extra lines, making lines at joints, points, and special features darker, and adding shading to show different textures.

An Ordinary Observation Becomes an Extraordinary Opportunity

Like many kids who live in the country, high school student Rachael Collier knew the easiest place to find monarch caterpillars was on the milkweed plants growing along the gravel roads near her home in Iowa. She noticed that the milkweed plants were often dusty, and she began to wonder if the road dust had any effect on the monarch larvae's health. Instead of waiting for someone else to answer her question, she turned a bathtub in her home into her laboratory, and started raising monarchs. Each day, she gave the same caterpillars milkweed plants that had a layer of road dust on them, and gave other caterpillars clean milkweed plants. She weighed the caterpillars at each stage of their development and kept track of how many lived and how many died. By the end, her records showed that monarch caterpillars exposed to limestone road dust were not as large and were more likely to die than caterpillars that ate clean milkweed. She presented her findings at science fair competitions, where she was awarded several thousand dollars in scholarship money, plus a summer research job in another country.

Make the Connection

If you really enjoy drawing insects, enter one of your artworks in the University of Illinois annual insect art contest. More information is available at www.life.uiuc.edu/entomology/egsa/ifff.html.

Although a journal and pencil are your most essential and valuable equipment, a few other things will make your study of insects easier and more fun. A magnifying lens is helpful for looking at very small insects, a ruler is important for noting the size of insects, and a jar where you can keep an insect from flying or crawling away while you are trying to sketch it is also handy. (Activities in chapter 5 will teach you how to catch insects, and chapter 6 has more information on making temporary insect homes.)

Rachael Collier's bathtub laboratory.

Courtesy of Rachael Collier

Looking Jar

Insect cages come in all sorts of shapes and sizes and are made from a wide variety of materials. While netting is good for airflow, it makes it hard to see the small details on insects. If you want to observe an insect for a short time, a clear, plastic container is your best bet.

Materials

A large, clear, plastic jar with a lid (large peanut butter containers work well)

Drill with very small bit (or a barbecue fork)

Insects need air to breathe, just like every other animal. To make your looking jar ready for temporary insect visitors, you need to make plenty of air holes.

However, many of the plastics used today are brittle and will split if you try to punch holes in them. With the help of an adult, you can either drill very small holes in the lid and near the bottom edge of the jar or heat the tip of the barbecue fork over a flame and melt small holes in the lid and near the bottom edge of the jar.

The larger the mouth of the jar, the easier it will be to put insects in. After you have watched your insects and made notes and sketches in your journal, turn the jar on its side and open the lid. Don't shake the jar to get the insects out, just wait a few minutes and they will be gone.

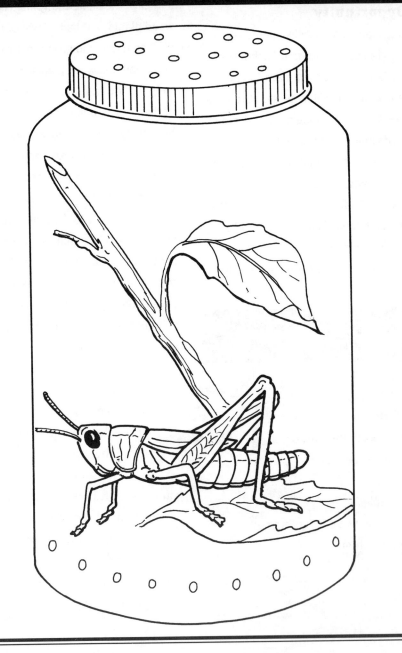

Field Research Tips

Many activities in this book should be done outdoors and with live insects. Since insects have a wide range of defense strategies, including biting, pinching, stinging, spraying, and spitting, here are a few tips and tricks to help you feel the most comfortable out in the field.

- If you are going to be collecting insects in tall grass or brushy areas, wear long, light-colored pants, a long-sleeved, light-colored shirt, closed-toe shoes, and a hat. These clothes will help protect you from scratches, scrapes, poison ivy, and insect attacks.
- It is a good idea to bring a simple first-aid kit with you. Tweezers, alcohol swabs, first-aid ointment, and bandages can be a big help.
- If you get stung by a bee, pull the stinger out immediately. To help ease the pain, put ice, baking soda, meat tenderizer, or barbecue sauce directly on top of the sting.
- Ticks are tiny creatures with eight legs. They can be as small as the size of a period to as big as the end of a pencil eraser. Most ticks need blood from a warm-blooded animal in order to continue their development or lay eggs. To discourage these bloodsucking ticks from feeding on you, tuck your pant legs into your socks. When you go inside, check all over your skin and in your hair to see if any ticks managed to sneak by. To remove a tick that is crawling on your clothes or skin, place the sticky side of a piece of tape on the tick. Lift up and fold the piece of tape in half (tick side in) to create your own piece of ticker tape. If a tick has its head stuck under your skin, have an adult use tweezers to remove it.

Do you have your journal and pencil ready? Are you dressed for adventure? Get ready to explore how insects are similar to and different from you as you attract, catch, study, mimic, and release insects in your area.

Body Basics

Put a butterfly and a cricket side by side, and what do you notice? Even though the size, shape, color, and sometimes the function of each part can be different, the basic body plan for both insects, and every other adult insect, is the same. (Immature insects can look very different than adult ones. See chapter 3, "Metamorphic Magic," for details.) They may seem similar to each other, but how do insects compare to you? Can they see better with those huge eyes? Are they really able to lift more, jump farther, and run faster than humans? Get ready to find out.

Insects are cold-blooded *invertebrates* (in-VUR-ta-brāts). Invertebrates are all animals that do not have a backbone, including worms, clams, slugs, and insects. Instead of having bones to hold their bodies up, insects have *exoskeletons*. Exoskeletons are like miniature suits of armor. These hard shells protect insects' bodies and give a place for their muscles to attach. However, a solid, hard shell would be too hard to bend and move, so insect bodies are divided into three parts, and each part has smaller segments.

The three body parts are the head, thorax, and abdomen.

On its head, an insect usually has two sets of jaws, two kinds of eyes, and one pair of antennae.

An insect's thorax has three segments. Each segment has a pair of jointed legs, so an insect normally has six legs. Most insects also have one pair of wings attached to the middle segment, and another pair of wings attached to the back segment. But some insects have only one pair of wings, and a few have none at all.

The abdomen is the softest and most flexible part of an insect's body. It usually has between eight and eleven segments with tiny holes called *spiracles* on the side of each segment. These holes are how an insect breathes. The abdomen also holds an insect's stomach and other organs.

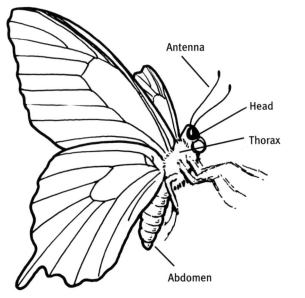

Antenna

Head

Thorax

Abdomen

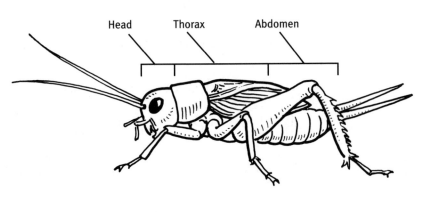

Head   Thorax   Abdomen

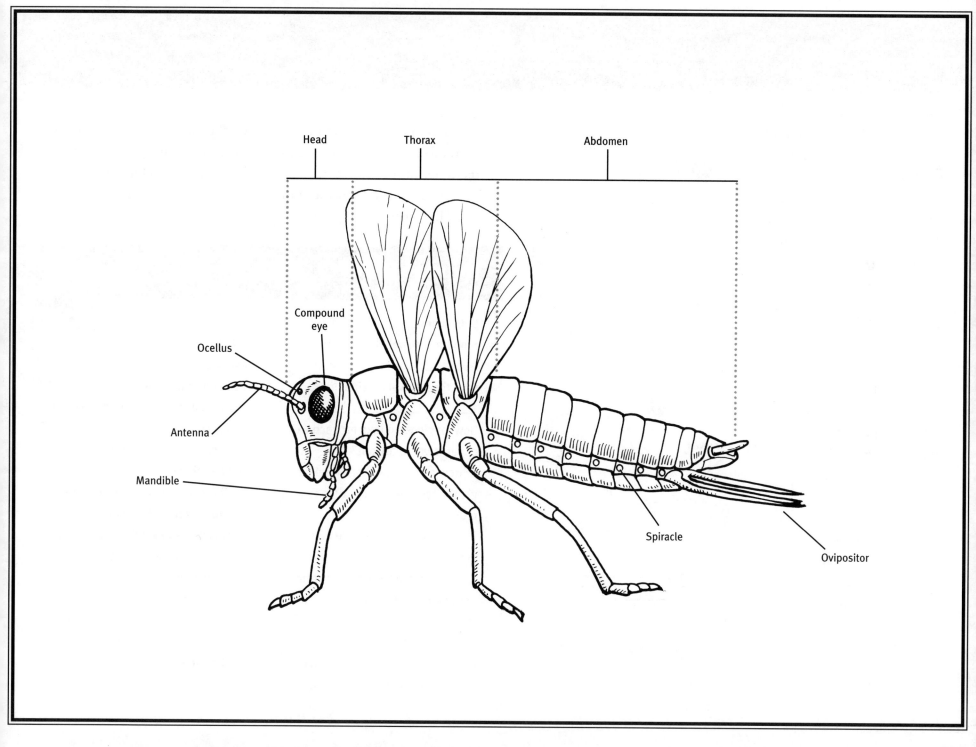

Head · Thorax · Abdomen

Compound eye

Ocellus

Antenna

Mandible

Spiracle

Ovipositor

Excellent Exoskeletons

Almost 300,000 kinds of beetles have been identified so far, making them the largest group of animals on the earth. Their hard exoskeletons are one reason they have been so successful. How do exoskeletons help beetles and other insects survive? This activity will give you some ideas.

Materials

Spray bottle with water
Paper towels
4 toilet paper tubes
Watch or clock
Red food coloring
Egg

Wet one paper towel and stuff it inside a toilet paper tube. Wet another paper towel and wrap it around the outside of a different tube. Record the time on your watch in your journal, then stand both tubes on end and set in a safe place. While these are drying,

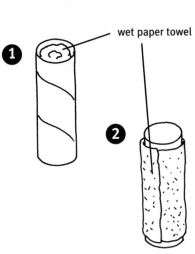

① wet paper towel

②

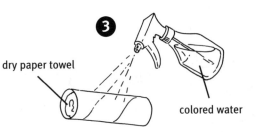

③ dry paper towel

colored water

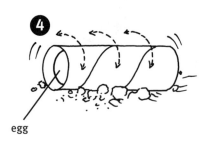

④

egg

stuff a dry paper towel inside a third tube. Add food coloring to the water in the spray bottle. Lay the tube down and spray it until color has seeped through the cardboard and stained the paper towel. Place an egg inside the fourth tube. Roll it across the ground until the egg breaks.

Journal Notes

Start time: _____
Stop time (towel inside dry):

_____

Stop time (towel outside dry):

_____

How long does it take for each wet paper towel to dry out?

How much spray does it take to get the towel inside the tube to turn red?

What finally causes the egg to break?

Our skin acts as a two-way transportation system. It lets water out (sweating), takes chemicals in (such as with skin lotion or medicine patches), and is easily bruised, scratched, and cut. Insect exoskeletons slow down water loss due to evaporation. They also keep unwanted chemicals (such as bug spray) from being taken in. Exoskeletons protect insects from cuts, scrapes, and bruises when they run into things.

There are two main disadvantages to exoskeletons. Every time an insect grows, it has to shed its skin. While it is shedding its exoskeleton, an insect's body is soft, making it easier for other animals to attack and eat it. And the exoskeleton limits how big an insect can get. You will never see a beetle the size of a small dog—the exoskeleton would be too heavy.

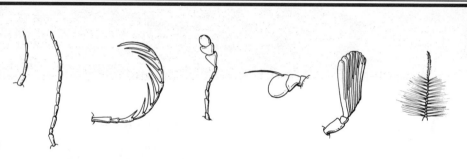

During the summer, the shed exoskeletons of cicadas (si-KĀ-das) can be found clinging to trees, fences, and even houses. While one type of cicada, known as dog day cicadas, appears each year, periodical cicadas live underground as nymphs for either 13 or 17 years.

Since worker honeybees do not mate and they often clamber into flowers to get nectar, honeybees have short, simple antennae. Moth antennae are often large and featherlike so they can detect small amounts of airborne chemicals to find a mate, but they don't get in the way since moths have long, tube-like mouthparts to obtain flower nectar. Can you determine other reasons for the different types of antennae?

Heads Up!

There are three main parts to an insect's head: the antennae, the eyes, and the mouth. How these three parts look and are used depends on what senses an insect needs to be successful where it lives. A cave cricket spends most of its time in caves, hollow trees, or under rocks. Being able to see well is not as important as being sensitive to smells and touches. So its eyes are very small, but its antennae are longer than its whole body. On the other hand, a fly has tiny antennae but its compound eyes take up two-thirds of its head. If a fly had a head the size of yours, its eyes would be about the size of cantaloupes. This lets a fly see almost all the way around its body without ever having to turn its head.

People use antennae on televisions, radios, and other electronic devices to get better signals. Insects use their antennae to get better signals, too. Insect antennae can be used to taste, touch, smell, and hear. There are at least 14 types of antennae. Antennae are different lengths and shapes, and have a different number of jointed segments. Entomologists often use the shape and the size of antennae to help them identify insects.

Insects have two kinds of eyes, simple and compound. In larvae, the simple eyes, called *ocelli* (ō-SEL-ī), can detect some colors and shapes, while the ocelli in adult insects are sensitive to light and movement but cannot see images.

It is the compound eyes on nymphs and adults that really see things. They are called compound eyes because each eye is made of between two and 23,000 lenses. Even with all these lenses, most insects are near-sighted—they can only see things that are pretty close to them. However, they can focus on things that we would need a microscope to see!

People use fingers, forks, spoons, straws, and cups to help get food into their mouths. While insects don't eat exactly the same way we do, they have mouthparts adapted to do many of the same jobs. These mouthparts determine the type of food an insect can eat.

A Plantastic Feast

A single plant can provide food for many different insects, with each kind feeding on a separate part of the plant. The coiled tube mouthpart of a butterfly is great for sipping nectar but is useless in trying to bite a green leaf. The chewing mouthparts of a grasshopper make a quick dinner of a leaf but can't pierce the stem to drink the sap. The piercing-sucking mouth of the spittlebug can do two jobs, first making a hole in the stem, then sucking out the plant juice, but can't soak up the juices that dribble down the side or spill on the ground. However, nothing goes to waste, as those juices are great for the sponging mouth of the fly.

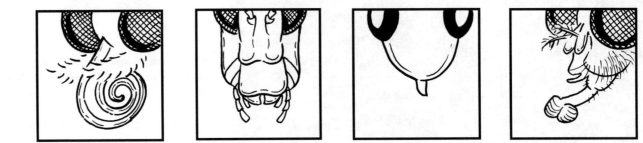

Because their mouthparts limit the types of food they can eat, most insects must be able to travel to find enough food.

Materials

Juice bag
Pointed-end straw (from the juice bag)
1 sheet of green construction paper
Tape
Sturdy plate (not paper)
Lettuce or spinach leaves
1 sheet of red construction paper
Pencil
Scissors
Small paper cup
Juice
2 Straws
Pliers
1 inch (2.5 cm) piece of clean sponge

Remove the straw from the juice bag. Wrap the sheet of green construction paper around the juice bag, tape it in place, and set it on the plate to create the stem of your plant. Tape the lettuce or spinach leaves to the side of your stem. Draw some flower petals on the red paper, cut them out, and tape them around the top rim of the small paper cup. Tape the cup to the back edge at the top of the stem and pour a bit of juice inside.

Now it is time for your plant to become dinner. Start out with a straw and take a butterfly sip of the nectar in the cup. Next, pick up the pliers and use them as a grasshopper would, ripping a leaf off the stem and taking it to your mouth. Use the pointed-end straw as your spittlebug mouth to jab a hole in the stem of your plant, then gently squeeze the stem as you sip some plant sap. To slurp up the juice that landed on the plate, put the sponge on the bottom of the straw. Move it around, then take your drink as a fly.

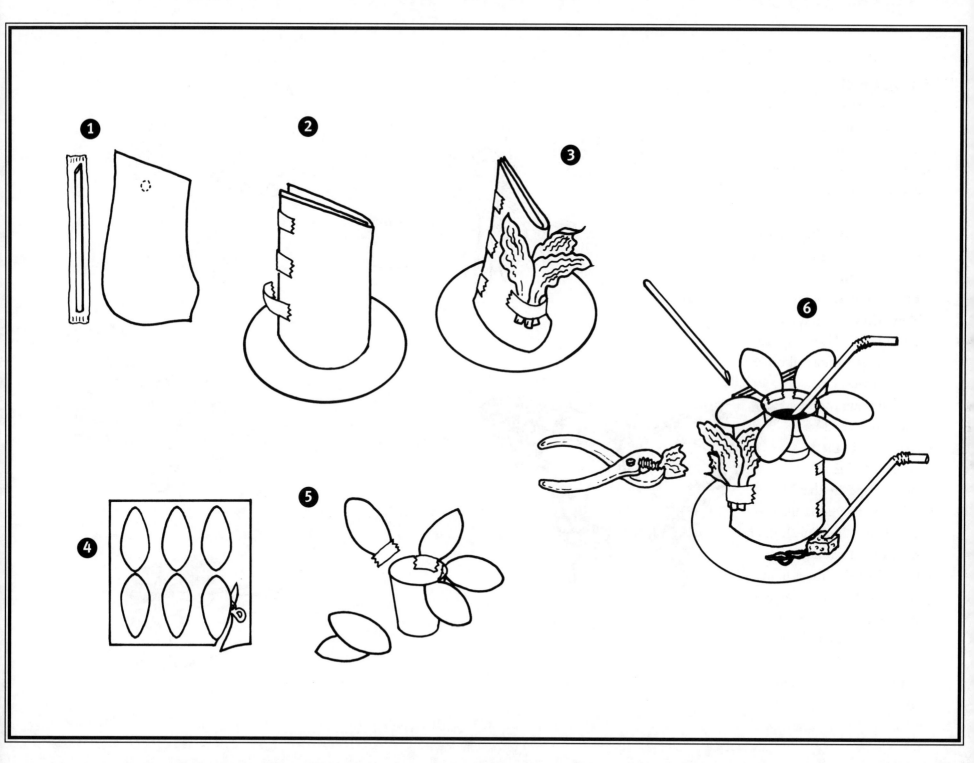

Thorax Up Close

Attached to the top of the thorax is the most noticeable part of many insects—the wings. Insects are the only types of invertebrates that have wings. Wings can be used to fly, to make sounds, and as protection. Wings also help entomologists identify the insects they catch.

Entomologists look to see:

- How many wings does the insect have? (Flies only have two wings. Almost all other flying insects have four, although some have none at all.)
- How big are the wings?
- What shape are they?
- What do they look like? Are they like cellophane, leather, scaly, or a hard shell?
- How does the insect hold its wings when it is not flying? Are they out to the side? Above its body like a tent? Tucked away?
- What do the wing veins look like?

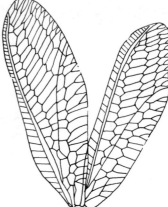
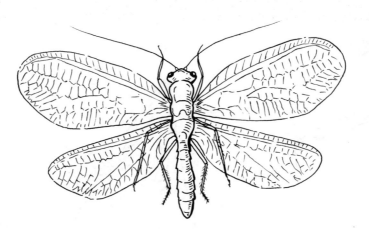

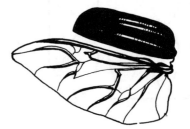

Need a Lift?

Many butterflies that travel long distances conserve their energy by gliding up and down, using invisible warm air bubbles, called thermals. When the sun shines on a dark parking lot surrounded by trees, the air over the parking lot gets much warmer than the air around the trees. Warm air is lighter than cooler air, so the warm air over the parking lot rises as a thermal. If a broad-winged butterfly flies by, it can stretch its wings and let the thermal carry it high into the sky, then glide down a long distance with just an occasional flap of its wings.

Materials

Sheet of thin writing paper
Pencil with sharp point
Scissors
Tissue paper
Index card

Trace the broad wing pattern onto the paper, making sure you include the dashed line. Cut it out around the solid line edge. Fold the paper along the dashed line to make a crease, then open it back up. Grab the pencil about halfway down in one hand. Use your other hand to balance the paper on the pencil tip. Hold steady for at least one minute and watch what happens. Trace the pattern on tissue paper and on an index card. What happens when you try to balance them? What happens if you make the pattern larger? Smaller? Stand on a chair and drop the wing pattern, noting what happens as it falls.

Journal Notes

I held the wing on the pencil point for one minute and this is what happened:

_____

When I did this with a thicker wing, this happened:

_____

When I did this with a thinner wing, this happened:

_____

When I dropped a wing from up high, this happened:

_____

What made the wing move? Your body makes heat. The heat from your hand created a mini-thermal that went up, hit the paper, and made it spin. When you dropped the paper, it likely twirled around as it fell, looking more like a maple seed or mini-helicopter than a gliding butterfly. One reason is because butterflies have four wings, not just two. The wings act together to control upward and downward motion, just like the flaps on a glider's wings.

Nervous Twitch

While some butterflies and moths flap slowly and gracefully as they float through the air, flies, bumblebees, and hummingbird moths flap faster than the eye can see. For years there has been a popular myth that bumblebees shouldn't be able to fly because they have a short, fat body shape and their nervous system can't send messages fast enough to make their wings flap the necessary 200 times a second. The truth behind the myth is that a bumblebee's shape and wings are more like a helicopter than a glider, and the muscles work a bit like a rubber band.

Materials

1 sheet of thin paper
Pencil with dull tip
Scissors
Foam tray or plate
Crayons
Thin rubber band

Place the sheet of thin paper over the bee and wing pattern and trace them. Cut them out, place them on the foam tray, and trace around them. Cut them out of the foam and decorate them with crayons. Place the rubber band over the bee pattern with the sides hooked into the notches. Put the wing piece in the middle of the rubber band. Wind the wing piece around 20 times in one direction. Release the wings, and watch and listen to them as they spin.

The nerves and thorax muscles that control a bumblebee's wings work in a somewhat similar manner. The muscles are ready to move, similar to you winding up the wings. Ten to twenty times a second, the nerves send the message to the wing muscles to flap, or in your case, to release the wings. It only takes one message from the nerves to get the wing muscles started, then they keep vibrating, like the rubber band keeps unwinding, moving the wings 10 to 20 times until the nerves send the next message to flap.

All About Legs

Legs are attached to the lower side of the thorax. Insect legs have the same basic parts that yours do, but many insects also have extra adaptations for survival. A praying mantis's front legs have sharp spines along the edges to hold its prey. Flies have sticky pads at the end of their legs to help them walk on things, even the ceiling. Grasshoppers and crickets have large bent hind legs, just right for jumping. Water boatmen and backswimmers have legs like oars for paddling through the water. Ground beetles have long, strong legs for running. And crane flies have very long legs, helping them stand above the grass on the ground.

About Abdomens

Abdomens can be long and thin, short and round, or shapes in between. Some are striped, some are one color, and some have little hooks at the end called *cerci* (SIR-sē). Bombardier beetles protect themselves by squirting boiling

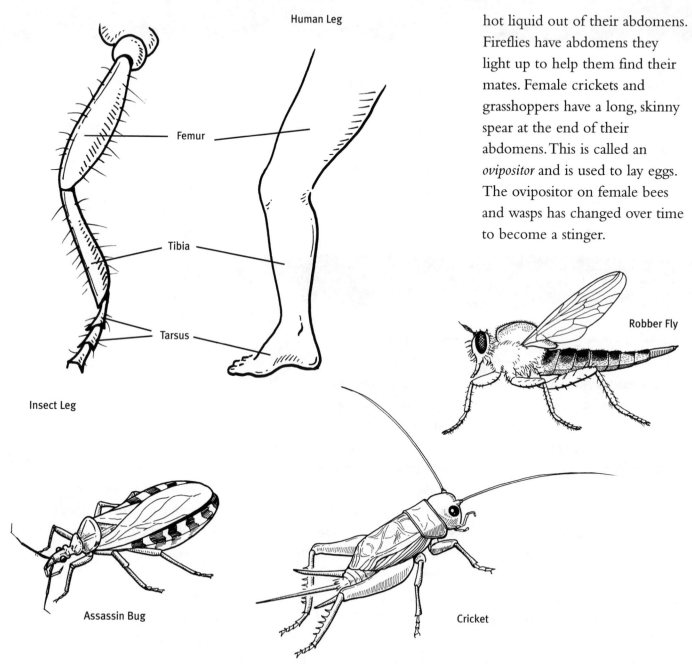

Human Leg

Femur

Tibia

Tarsus

Insect Leg

Robber Fly

Assassin Bug

Cricket

hot liquid out of their abdomens. Fireflies have abdomens they light up to help them find their mates. Female crickets and grasshoppers have a long, skinny spear at the end of their abdomens. This is called an *ovipositor* and is used to lay eggs. The ovipositor on female bees and wasps has changed over time to become a stinger.

Mighty Muscles

Have you heard of the amazing feats that insects can do? Ants can lift 50 times their own body weight. Grasshoppers can jump 30 times their body length. If you were to compete against insects in Olympic events, how well would you do?

Since you are much larger than insects, of course you can lift more actual weight than an ant, and jump higher and farther than a flea. To make the contests fair, you need to relate how far and high you jump, how fast you run, and how much you can lift to your own body size.

Materials
Tape measure
Pencil
Bathroom scale
Chalk
Rope
Watch with a second hand
Friends

Record your height in inches (or centimeters) and your weight in pounds (or kilograms) in your journal, then get ready to do your best!

Draw a line on the ground with the chalk. From a still position, jump as far as you can. Mark where you landed. Measure how far you jumped. Divide this number by your height to determine how many body lengths you jumped.

Tie a rope between two trees or solid posts, about eight inches (20 cm) above and parallel to the ground. Try to jump over the rope without taking a running start. If you make it over, raise the rope two inches (5 cm). Keep raising the height until you miss

This female rhinoceros beetle moved nearly 100 times its own mass during an experiment measuring how much energy it used while carrying extra weight.

Photograph courtesy of Rodger Kram, Ph.D., University of Colorado

Bug Business

Fireflies, which are a family of beetles, can be found on every continent except Antarctica, but not every firefly flashes. In the United States, the fireflies that live east of the Rocky Mountains and away from the desert Southwest flash their abdominal lights on warm summer nights.

While most people catch fireflies for fun, some people do it for money. Since 1952, a company in Tennessee has sponsored a summer firefly drive. It pays people to catch and freeze fireflies. The company collects these fireflies, then sells them to researchers. The researchers remove the chemical that glows (luciferin) and use it in their studies. Some researchers mix the luciferin with small samples of ground beef or other foods. If the bacteria *e. coli* is in the food, the luciferin attaches to the bacteria, making it easy for researchers to see it.

How much do firefly catchers earn? The price can change, but a good estimate is about one penny per perfect insect.

it three times in a row. Record the highest level you jumped in your journal. Divide this number by your height to determine how many body lengths high you jumped.

Begin from a still position at a starting line. Run as fast as you can for five seconds (have a friend use a watch to time your run). Measure how far you ran in inches (cm) and record this number in your journal. Divide this number by 5 to determine how far you ran per second. Divide how far you ran per second by your height to figure out how many body lengths that is.

Gather some friends who weigh about the same amount as you. Put your hands and knees on the ground, keeping your back in the air. Ask your friends to straddle your back, adding one more friend at a time until you cannot hold any more without collapsing.

Record Holders

Event	Long jump	High jump	Running	Lifting
Human	About 29.5 feet (almost 9 meters) = about 4.5 body lengths	Over 8 feet (2.4 m) (with a running start) = about 1.25 x height	About 20 miles (32 km) per hour = between 5 and 6 body lengths per second	17 x body weight in a trestle lift
Insect	A 2-inch (5 cm) grasshopper can jump 30 inches (76 cm) = 15 body lengths	0.1 inch (.25 cm) cat flea has jumped 13 inches (33 cm) = 130 x its height	Cockroaches run about 3.7 miles (6 km) per hour = 50 body lengths per second	Rhinoceros beetle can support 850 times its own weight on its back

Journal Notes

Write these sentences into your journal and fill in the blanks with your results.

I am _____(A) inches/cm tall and I weigh _____ pounds/kg.

1. I jumped a distance of _____(B) inches/cm.
B ÷ A = _____ is the number of body lengths long that I jumped.

2. I jumped _____(C) inches/cm high.
C ÷ A = _____ is the number of body lengths high that I jumped.

3. I ran _____(D) inches/cm in 5 seconds.
D ÷ 5 = _____(E) distance per second.
E ÷ A = _____ is the number of body lengths per second I jumped.

4. I can hold _____ friends on my back at the same time.

Who wins every contest? Don't feel bad that the insects always win. For one thing, many insects have more muscles than we do. Humans have about 800 muscles. Grasshoppers have about 900 and caterpillars have as many as 4,000!

Rigged Ratios

Not only do insects have more muscles, but those muscles have to do less work. When muscles work, they have to move whatever is being lifted or pushed and the body parts as well. Since humans have more inside (volume) compared to their skin (surface area) than insects do, our muscles have a bigger job to do from the start.

Materials
Pencil
2 pieces of paper (8½ × 11 inches)
Tape
2 pieces of stiff cardboard
Dry cereal

Sketch a strong insect (an ant or beetle is a good choice) on one piece of paper, and a human on the other. Roll the insect paper along the long edge to form a tall tube, and tape the sides. Roll the human paper along the short edge to form a shorter tube, and again, and tape the sides. Place one of the tubes on a piece of stiff cardboard and fill it to the top with dry cereal.

Place the other tube on the other piece of cardboard. Pour the cereal from the first tube into the second one.

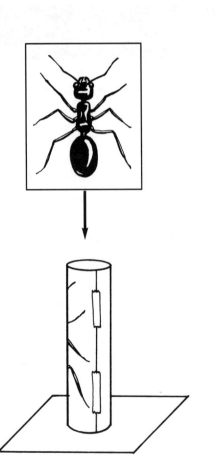

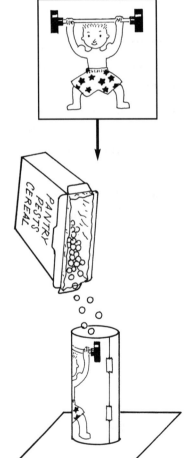

Journal Notes

The _____ tube held the greater amount (volume) of dry cereal.

You started with the same size paper, so each tube has the same surface area. But because of the way you rolled the paper, one tube holds a greater volume than the other. This is true when you compare insect and human bodies as well. Because of the way they are made, insects have less volume compared to their surface area than humans do.

Even though you have a greater volume compared to your surface area than an insect does, and an insect has more muscles than you do, if you found an insect the same size as you, you would likely have about equal strength.

What's Bugging You?

Entomologists use everything from an insect's antennae to its toes to help identify each kind. Insects that look and act a lot alike are put in big groups called orders. All the butterflies and moths are grouped together in one order, beetles are another order, and cockroaches are a third order. There are about 30 major orders of insects. You will most likely be able to find insects from around ten of these orders. These ten common orders and their characteristics are listed at the end of the book in the table titled "Ten Common Insect Orders" (see page 117).

Classification

Around 1735, Carolus Linnaeus introduced a new system of classification—a way to identify, name, and group living things in an organized way. Although his first system concentrated on plants, he later worked to organize animals into a formal system as well. There are seven major levels of information used to classify all living things.

The system works like making a seven-level name and address for each living thing. Each level of information gets more specific. Imagine you were space-traveling in a distant galaxy and met another creature who asked where you were from. If the creature wanted your exact address, you might answer something like: Milky Way Galaxy, Planet Earth, North American continent, United States of America, State of Iowa, City of Des Moines, 1234 Main Street.

The first level of information in the name address for a living organism is called the Kingdom. There is a Plant Kingdom, an Algae Kingdom, a Fungi Kingdom, and, of course, an Animal Kingdom. All animals are part of the Animal Kingdom, so it is a very big group.

As scientists look at all the different kinds of animals, they sort them into smaller, more exclusive groups called Phyla. Furry, warm-blooded animals with backbones who give birth to live babies and feed them milk are put in the Mammals phylum, while those animals with exoskeletons, at least two body segments, and pairs of jointed legs are in the *Arthropod* (ARE-thrō-pod) phylum.

Insects are members of the Arthropod phylum, as are spiders, centipedes, and lobsters. So scientists take all the animals in the Arthropod phylum and sort them into even smaller groups, called classes. All six-legged arthropods are put in the insect class, while the other arthropods are put into different classes like the arachnid (spider) class or the crustacea (lobster, crabs) class.

Scientists keep sorting each level into smaller and smaller groups. All the animals in each class are put into orders. Bugs, beetles, and flies are all in different orders. Each order is sorted into smaller groups called families. Stinkbugs, assassin bugs, and bedbugs are all in different families. Each family is sorted into a small group called a genus (JîN-us). Stinkbugs could belong to the rough stinkbug genus, the green stinkbug genus, or one of several others, with each group having only a few members. Finally, at the very end, each animal gets its very own name; that is, its species. The species name for the spined soldier stinkbug is *Podisus maculiventris*. If you put together all the classification information about the spined soldier stinkbug, this is what it would look like:

Classification Level	Animals Included
Kingdom Animalia	All animals
Phylum Arthropoda	Only those animals with jointed legs, two or more body segments, exoskeleton
Class Insecta	Only those arthropods with six legs, two antennae
Order Hemiptera	Only those insects with front wings longer than hind wings, and a piercing-sucking mouth that forms a beak
Family Pentatomidae	Only those bugs with a shield-shaped back and strong, defensive odor
Genus *Podisus*	Only those stinkbugs considered soldier stinkbugs
Species *maculiventris*	The spined soldier stinkbug

What tools can you use to figure out which order an insect belongs to? There are two basic types of books to help you: field guides and keys. Field guides include pictures of the insects, common names, and a short description. You can find a field guide that includes all different kinds of the most common insects, or one for just one type of insect, such as butterflies. To identify an insect, you look through the field guide to find the picture that looks the most like what you have found.

A key is a list that gives you two choices. After picking the choice that best describes your insect, you follow the instructions to the next set of choices.

First Field Guides

Field guides come in many different shapes and sizes. Some use photographs of insects; some use detailed black and white drawings; others use colored illustrations. Look at several different types of field guides to find the one that is right for you. The field guides listed here are first guides. To keep them light and easy-to-use, they only include the insects you are most likely to find.

Bugs and Slugs: An Introduction to Familiar Invertebrates. Pocket Naturalist by James Kavanagh (Waterford Press, Inc., 2002).

Insects: A Concise Field Guide to 200 Common Insects of North America. Peterson's First Guides by Christopher Leahy (Houghton Mifflin, 1987).

Insects: A Guide to Familiar American Insects. A Golden Guide by Herbert S. Zim, Ph.D. and Clarence Cottam, Ph.D. (Golden Press, 1987).

Insects and Spiders: National Audubon Society's Pocket Guide (Chanticleer Press Inc., 1988).

Insects: Spiders and Other Terrestrial Arthropods. Dorling Kindersley Handbooks by George C. McGavin (Dorling Kindersley Inc., 2000).

For example, a key to put an insect in the right order might start out like this:

1. Does the adult have well-developed wings?

   Yes (go to 2)   No (go to 28)

2. Are the wings clear?

   Yes (go to 3)   No (go to 24)

3. Are there two sets of clear wings?

   Yes (go to 4)   No (go to 20)

After going through a list and picking the best descriptions, your final choice tells you to which order your insect belongs. If you want to find out which family, genus, and species your insect belongs to, you use another key that is made for each order. Keys are usually found in entomology textbooks and other scientific resources.

While most amateur entomologists start by using field guides, it doesn't matter which type of book you use. After some practice, you will be able to automatically put most insects into the right order.

Don't get discouraged if you have trouble identifying some insects you find. Sometimes it takes professional entomologists days or weeks to identify an insect all the way to its species name. After comparing an unknown insect to similar ones in their collections, entomologists use a microscope to look at its antennae, mouthparts, how the wings are veined, and other very specific details. Even then, they are sometimes fooled. Everyone agreed that a certain insect in Borneo looked and acted like a tiger beetle. It was only when one entomologist started to raise the insect from an egg to adult that he became suspicious. Beetles undergo complete metamorphosis, but this insect did not. He finally determined that the insect was actually a grasshopper, acting like a beetle. Very tricky!

Make a Connection

Go to www.csrees.usda.gov/ Extension/ or look in the phone book for your area Cooperative State Research, Education and Extension Service (look for Extension Service in the county government section). Many of them have active entomology departments that will identify insects found in your state.

What's in a Name?

People often call the same insect by different names. For example, do you call it a lightning bug or a firefly? To make sure they are all talking about the same insect, entomologists use the official two-part name for each insect. The first part of the name is the genus, which puts each insect into a small group of very similar insects. The second part is the species name, which tells you exactly which insect you have. It works a lot like your name when it is listed in a phone book. Your last name (surname) groups you with the other members of your family. Your first name shows exactly which family member you are.

If you use a key to identify the insects you catch, you will see the official names. The official names are usually in Latin, and some are hard to pronounce, like *Drosophila melangaster* (fruit fly). Of course, some entomologists have fun, even with Latin names. G.W. Kirkaldy named one bug *Ochisme* (o-kiss-me), another one *Polychisme* (Polly-kiss-me), and a third one *Marichisme* (Mary-kiss-me). A fly was named *Pieza kake* (piece of cake), and one entomologist named a moth *Dyaria* (which sounds the same as diarrhea).

Insect Imposters

Insects, spiders, centipedes, millipedes, ticks, scorpions, mites, and lobsters all belong to the Arthropod phylum, a very large group of animals. Many arthropods live close to each other, sometimes under the same rock or in the same rotting log. Its no wonder people often get confused by the different types of small, many-legged creatures and just call them all "bugs." Turn the page to find some clues to help you separate real insects from their close cousins, the insect imposters.

Common Names

Many insects have a common name in addition to their scientific name. The common name is like a nickname and often describes the insect. Honeybee, walking stick, grasshopper, fire ant, stinkbug, and swallowtail butterfly are examples of common names. How many other ones can you think of?

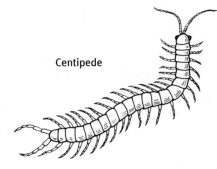

Centipede

Centipedes: long, flat bodies with 15 to 181 segments. The one pair of legs on each body segment stretches out to the side.

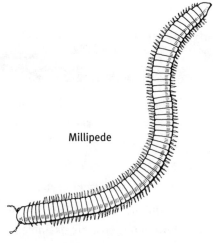

Millipede

Millipedes: cylinder-like body with 9 to 100+ segments. Each segment has two pairs of legs, which are directly under the body.

Sowbug

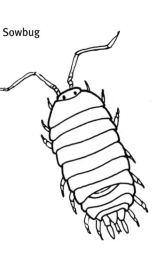

Isopods (pill bugs or roly-polies): two body parts, hard shell, one pair of antennae, and usually five or more pairs of legs.

Mite

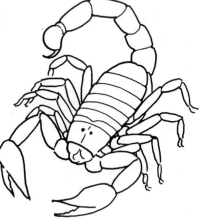

Scorpion

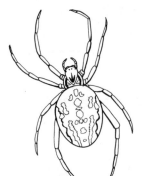

Spiders

Arachnids: spiders, mites, ticks, and scorpions. Eight legs, two body segments, and no antennae.

Tick

Twist–an–Insect (Game Dice)

The classification orders put insects with parts that go together in predictable ways in the same group. Flies have two wings and sponging mouthparts. Grasshoppers have large hind legs for jumping and chewing mouthparts. Beetles have a line that goes straight down their back, and many have a set of pinching jaws called *mandibles*.

By making and using a twist-an-insect, you will start to recognize characteristics that go together. This will make it easier to classify anything you catch to the right order.

Materials

3 photocopies or tracings of cube pattern on page 28
1 photocopy or tracing of insects on page 29 and page 30
Scissors
Pencil or hole punch
Markers/colored pencils

Glue stick
Thin dowel rod (¼ inch [⁶⁄₁₀ cm] diameter), 7 inches (17.75 cm) long
Pencil topper erasers (optional)

Carefully cut along the thick black outer lines on the cube pattern. Fold and crease along all the thinner inner lines, then flatten the pattern again. Use your pencil point or a hole punch to poke through the circles. Do this for all three copies of the cube. Color the insect pictures on pages 29 and 30. Cut along the dotted lines. Glue all the head pieces, one picture per square, on one cube pattern; all the thorax pieces, one picture per square, on a second cube pattern; and all the abdomen pieces, one picture per square, on a third cube pattern. When the glue has dried, use your pencil point or punch to poke through the circles again. Put glue on the trapezoid tab pieces and fold the pieces up, sticking the tabs on the inside, to form a cube. It is easiest to do the long side last. Place the cubes on the dowel rod with the head box on top, the thorax box in the middle and the abdomen box on the bottom. Put pencil top erasers over the ends of the rod to keep the boxes in place. Twist the boxes around to create a crazy creature or to help identify insects that you catch. When you want to play the Insectigations! game, take the boxes off the sticks to use them as dice.

Animal	Head: Feeding parts, eyes, and antennae	Thorax: Legs, wings	Abdomen: Shape and other features
Bee	Coiled tube mouthparts, medium compound eyes, short antennae	Four clear wings, small legs with pollen baskets	Striped, squat, hairy, stinger
Cricket	Chewing mouthparts, long antennae, small compound eyes	Large hind legs bent higher than the body; four wings held to sides when resting	Long, thick, females have ovipositor, males have claspers (cerci) at end
House Fly	Sponging mouth, very large compound eyes, short antennae	Two clear wings, hairy body, walking legs	Short, round, soft, hairy
Stag Beetle	Small eyes, mouth with pincers, long antennae	Running legs, two pairs of wings, hard wing shell makes middle line down back.	Abdomen hidden by shell
Moth	Feathery antennae, coiled tube mouthparts, small compound eyes	Four colored wings with scales	Fat, fuzzy, long abdomen
Spider	Eight simple eyes, no antennae	Eight legs on combined head and thorax	Soft, hairy abdomen with six spinnerets

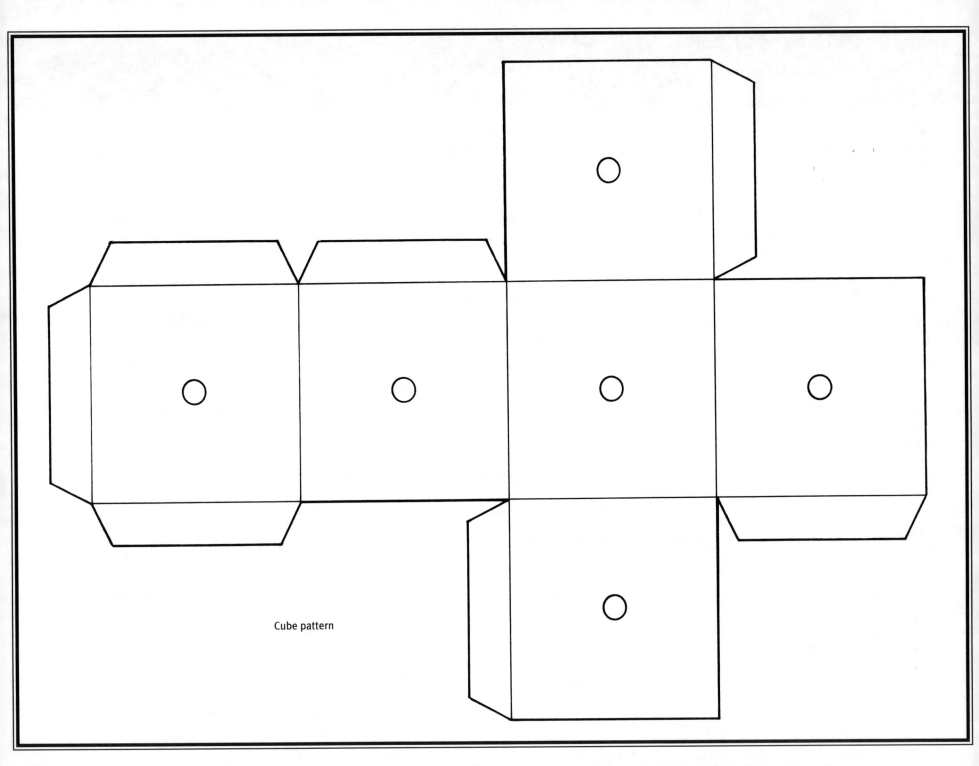

Cube pattern

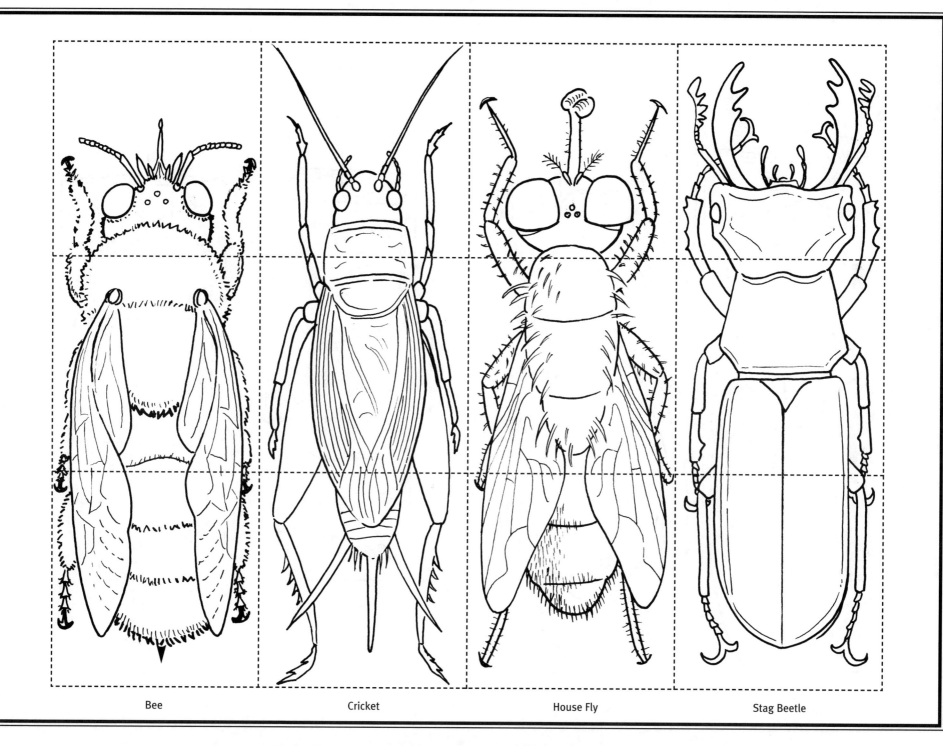

Bee   Cricket   House Fly   Stag Beetle

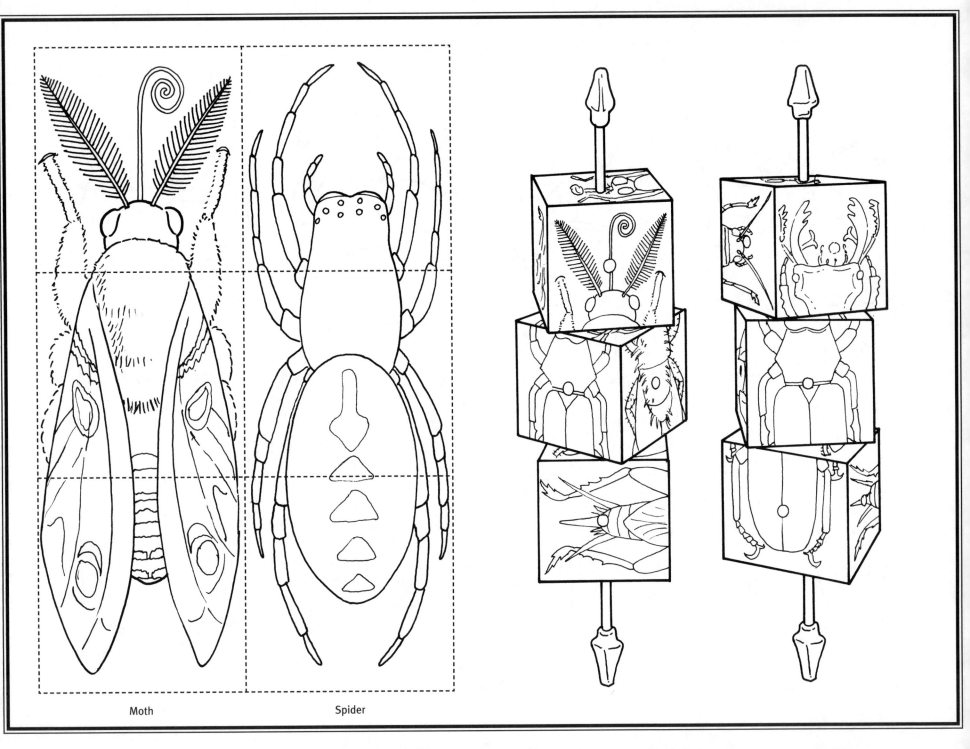

Moth

Spider

Insectigations! Game Action Cards

Being an insect has its advantages and drawbacks. While food is usually easy to find, predators are almost always lurking nearby. You will get to test your luck at surviving as an insect in the *Insectigations!* game included on page 115, but first you need to create action cards. Action cards will be used to build the path, with instructions for moving your game token forward and backward as you try to be the first player to make it from egg to adult.

Materials

2 3-by-5-inch (7.6-by-12.7-cm)
    index cards
Scissors
Pen
Envelope

Cut the index cards in half so that you have 4 2½-by-3-inch (6.3-by-7.6-cm) cards. Write the following actions based on insect anatomy onto the cards, one per card. Place all four cards (including the blank one) into the envelope for safekeeping until you are ready to create your *Insectigations!* game.

• You stumbled across a picnic! Roll the head die. If you have mandibles to carry away the crumbs, roll again.
• A hungry bird is looking for an easy meal. If a roll of the abdomen die shows you have an unprotected abdomen, go back to start.
• Here comes a fly swatter! If a roll of the head die doesn't show big compound eyes, lose one turn.

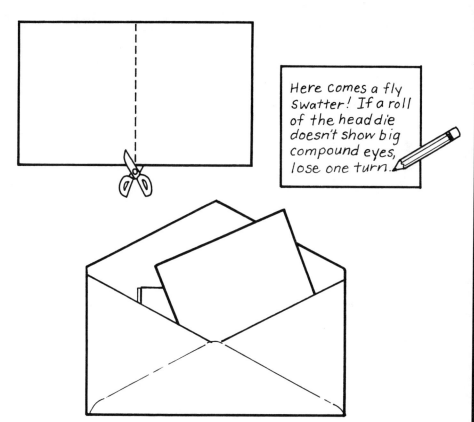

Here comes a fly swatter! If a roll of the head die doesn't show big compound eyes, lose one turn.

Although adult insects come in many shapes, sizes, and colors, at least they all have the same basic body plan. On the other hand, immature insects often look very different from each other, and even from their parents. Get ready to explore and understand metamorphosis, one of nature's greatest magic shows.

3

Metamorphic Magic

Most animals are born with all the body parts they will ever have and in the *habitat* where they will spend their whole lives. As animals grow bigger, they might grow fur or feathers, and move to a new place within a habitat, but most animals look and act pretty much the same their whole life.

Insects are different. Insects change. This process of change is called *metamorphosis* (met-a-MŌR-fa-sis). Soft, white, worm-like grubs that hatch from their eggs will later emerge from stiff pupal cases as beautifully colored hard-shelled beetles. Striped caterpillars that creep along munching green leaves become winged butterflies, flying through the air and feeding on flower nectar. Algae-eating mayfly nymphs that breathe underwater through gills surface from the bottom of a pond or stream, split their skins, stretch their iridescent wings and fly away, never to eat again.

Spontaneous Generation

Hundreds of years ago, people didn't know where living things came from. They believed that frogs came from mud along the rivers, mice grew from spoiled grain, and flies grew out of rotting meat hanging in a butcher's shop. The idea that living creatures came from non-living items was called spontaneous generation.

Francesco Redi wasn't sure whether he believed in spontaneous generation or not. So in 1668, he did an experiment to see if fly maggots really came from meat.

Materials

3 pieces of raw meat the size of a meatball
3 clear containers, 1 with a tight lid
Large piece of gauze
Rubber band

Put one piece of meat in each container. Leave one container open, close another one with the tight lid, and place a piece of gauze over the top of the third container, using the rubber band to hold it in place.

Place all three containers outside in an area where insects can get to them, but animals like dogs, cats, or raccoons can't.

Journal Notes

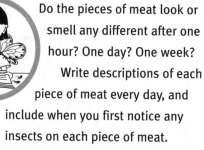

Do the pieces of meat look or smell any different after one hour? One day? One week?

Write descriptions of each piece of meat every day, and include when you first notice any insects on each piece of meat.

Do any changes affect all three pieces of meat?

What caused the changes?

What did Francesco see? He noticed flies landed on the meat in the open bottle, and flies landed on the gauze covering the second bottle.

No flies visited the meat in the bottle with the lid. Several days later, the meat left in the open was covered with maggots. The piece covered with gauze had just a few maggots. The piece in the closed bottle had nothing on it. After many more days, the maggots changed into flies.

Francesco had found his answer. He spread the word that flies didn't start from the meat itself, but came from other flies that visited the meat and laid eggs. Did your results match Francesco's?

Complete Metamorphosis

Most insects, including butter-flies, bees, beetles, ants, fleas, flies, and wasps, go through the process of complete metamorphosis. These insects change so much between the egg and adult stages that it is hard to believe they are really the same animals.

It starts when a female lays an egg. Most eggs are laid on or near the type of food the young eat. When the insect hatches, it usually looks like a soft worm and is called a first instar larva.

Butterfly and moth larvae = caterpillars

Legless fly larvae = maggots

Beetle and bee larvae = grubs

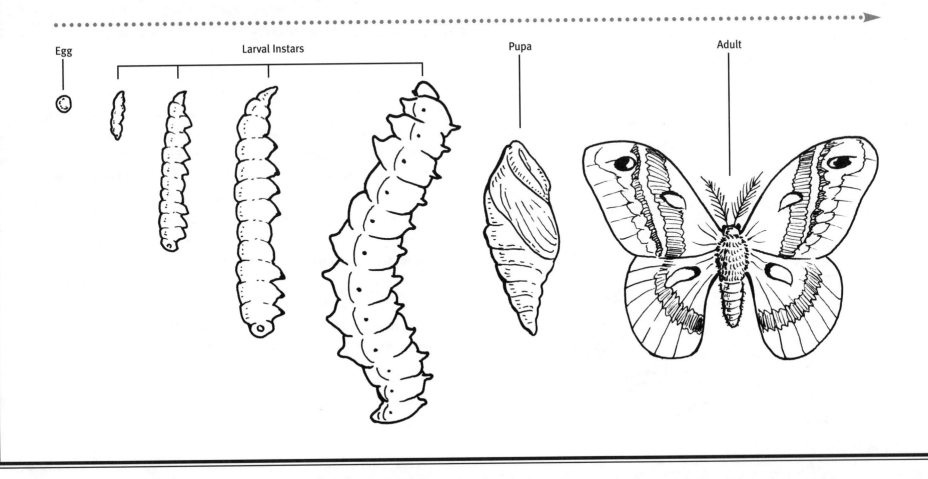

Egg   Larval Instars   Pupa   Adult

Almost immediately, the larva starts eating and growing. Although the skin is soft, it can only stretch so far. Once the larva has grown too large for its skin, it molts, shedding its skin. Now it is a second instar larva. It eats and grows some more. Depending on the insect, there are usually between five and seven instars.

After the final instar, the larva moves to a protected area and pupates (PYOO-pātes). Some insects, like butterflies and moths, spin a silken cocoon around themselves as protection during their pupation. Flies keep their next-to-the-last-shed skin on their bodies. As it dries, it forms a hard case. Beetles, ants, and bees pupate looking a bit like mummified adults. The pupal stage can last a few weeks, a few months, or even years! During pupation, the insect doesn't move around on the outside, but its insides are

Make a Connection

To view a computer-animated version of the complete metamorphosis of a butterfly, go to: www.bijlmakers.com/entomology/metamorphosis.htm.

going topsy-turvy. The body tissues dissolve and reorganize: growing legs, forming wings, developing compound eggs, adding hard shells, changing mouthparts. When the

adult insect finally emerges, it will not grow or change any more. In fact, some adult insects don't even have mouths that work, so they can't eat. The main job for adult insects is to find mates so that new eggs can be laid and the cycle can start all over again.

Metamorphic Records

Here are some amazing metamorphic examples.

- To take advantage of temporary pools of water, mosquitoes can go from egg to adult in as little as eight days.
- When droughts dry up the soils in Africa, the midge larvae dry up as well. They can survive dehydration

for three or more years, waiting for soaking rains to restart their metamorphosis.

- One species of periodical cicada spends 17 years as a nymph underground.
- Living in the Arctic means that caterpillars are active for only a few weeks each summer. This causes some moths to live 14

years as a caterpillar before spinning a cocoon.

- Woodboring beetles have emerged as adults 10 to 26 years after the wood they were living in was used for walls, floors, doors, and stairway handrails.
- One hundred eighty yucca moths emerged from their cocoons 16 to 17 years after they first spun them.

Raising Mealworms

Mealworms are one of the easiest animals to raise from egg to adult to egg again. Mealworms earned their name because they are often found in containers of cornmeal and cereal. In nature, they can be found under rocks or the bark of rotting logs. If you don't want to go on a mealworm hunt through your house or backyard, you can pick some up at a pet store where they sell them as food for reptiles and amphibians.

Materials

A clear shoe box or food keeper
    with a lid
Oatmeal or bran cereal
Potato, carrot or apple slices
Mealworms
Fine-tip permanent markers of
    various colors
Ruler

Poke a lot of small holes in the lid of the box. Spread an inch or

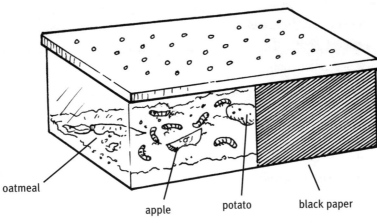

oatmeal
apple
potato
black paper

two of oatmeal or bran cereal on the bottom to provide food for both the larvae and adults. Since these insects get their water from the food they eat, add a slice of potato, carrot, or apple. Be sure to replace these every few days so you don't grow mold instead of mealworms! Add the mealworms to the box.

The larvae will be more active if you keep them in a warm (between 70° to 80°F [52° to 62°C]), dark place, but light and cooler temperatures will not hurt them. In nature, it can take nine

months or more for mealworms to complete a life cycle. In your box, it will probably take only between 76 and 136 days. Mealworms hatch from their eggs after about six to 14 days, grow and molt as larvae for 60 to 120 days, pupate for about 10 days, and finally emerge as adult darkling beetles. Use fine tip permanent markers to make a small dot or two on mealworm eggs and larvae. For example, eggs laid on July 7 might have one orange dot while eggs laid on July 9

might have one orange dot and one blue dot. Record your color code in your journal to help you keep track of the development of each egg and larva.

Journal Notes

Here is my color code:

_____

How long did each stage last?

How long (in inches or centimeters) is each instar larva?

How many instars does a mealworm go through?

What color is the adult when it first emerges from the pupa? What color is it after one hour? One day?

When you have finished studying the mealworms, you can feed the eggs, larvae, and adults to the fish, frogs, and turtles at a local pond.

Simple Metamorphosis

Several familiar insects, including grasshoppers, crickets, dragonflies, cicadas, and box elder bugs undergo simple (sometimes called incomplete) metamorphosis. Some of these insects change only a little; others change a lot. What they have in common is that they never have a resting period of pupation; instead they change as they grow. There are several different types of simple metamorphosis.

A young grasshopper hatches out of an egg and is called a nymph. It looks a lot like a mature grasshopper, except it is smaller and has short wing stubs. It eats and eats and eats. When it gets too big for its skin, it molts, leaving the old skin behind. The wings develop a bit more with each molt. After about six molts, it is an adult. It cannot grow or shed its skin anymore, but it continues to eat the same plant food and lives in the same habitat.

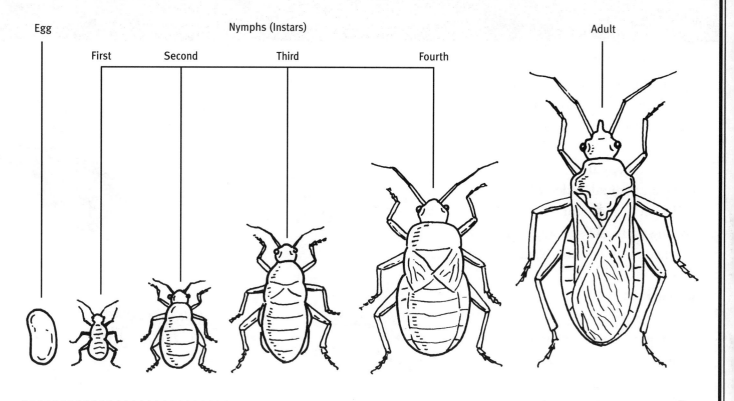

Egg

Nymphs (Instars)

First   Second   Third   Fourth

Adult

A dragonfly hatches underwater as short, squat, gill-breathing naiad with simple eyes. For the next two or three years, as it eats small aquatic animals, grows, and molts, its body is changing inside. Before its final molt, it climbs out of the water and onto a plant stem. As it sheds its last skin, it emerges with a long slender body, limp, wet wings, and huge compound eyes. After its wings have stretched, dried, and hardened, the adult dragonfly flies off in search of a mosquito—or another flying insect—for dinner, and leaves behind its watery home.

Searching for Insect Eggs

inding and raising insects from their eggs is a great way to learn more about metamorphosis. You can look for eggs almost any time of the year. Look on the underside of leaves, under rocks and rotting logs, floating on top of still water, or attached to underwater plants.

Materials

Clear containers
Damp paper towel or sponge
Jar lid

Do not pick up any insect egg by itself. Gently scoop it up with some of the surrounding soil, plant, or water, and place it in a clear container. Place a damp paper towel or sponge on a jar lid inside the container with any eggs that are not already in water. It is best to keep the eggs in a

safe place outside. You don't want to accidentally release a swarm of hungry, biting larvae in your house! And insect eggs found in the fall or winter might need to be exposed to cold temperatures in order to develop. Check on the eggs every day and note what happens.

Journal Notes

Where did you find the eggs?
Were there any adult insects around?

How long did it take for the eggs to hatch?
Can you identify the larvae?

Praying mantises enclose their eggs in a case of froth, then leave them to last through the winter.

Real Entomologists

Forensic entomologists use insect metamorphosis to help solve crimes. When forensic entomologists examine a dead body, they look for signs of insects. It is very hard to identify different types of fly and beetle eggs, larvae, shed skins and pupae, or tell how old they are, so forensic entomologists take samples back to their laboratories. They tend the eggs, feed the larvae, or watch the pupae until the adult insects emerge. After identifying them, they use their knowledge of metamorphosis to figure out when the eggs were first laid. By looking at how long each stage lasted, then counting backward, forensic entomologists get valuable clues on how long the body had been dead.

Crop specialists use their knowledge of metamorphosis to control pest insects. Many caterpillars eat plants. Too many caterpillars in a garden or farm can reduce the amount of food that plants can produce. One way to control the caterpillars is to release wasps which lay their eggs inside the caterpillars. When the eggs hatch, the larvae eat the insides of the caterpillar, then burrow outside to pupate.

Veterinarians need to know about metamorphosis to help sick animals. Horse bot flies lay eggs on horses' legs and shoulders. When horses lick their fur, they swallow the eggs. The eggs hatch inside the horse where the larvae feed and grow until they are ready to pupate. Then they let go and get passed out with the poop. Too many larvae inside a horse can make it very sick.

Gross Entomology:
What's for Dinner, Mom?

In one species of gall gnats, the mother gnat might not lay eggs. Instead, she produces female larvae inside her body. These daughters eat the insides of their own mother, then crawl out of her empty body. After these larvae molt (and are now second instar larvae), they all produce even more female larvae inside their own bodies, get eaten alive by their daughters, and then die when the daughters crawl out. This can happen several more times before one generation of the larvae don't produce any more daughters inside their bodies, but finally pupate and become true adults.

This tobacco hornworm is covered with pupal cases of braconid wasps.

Robert L. Anderson, USDA Forest Service. Image 1748031. www.ipmimages.org

Action Cards

Materials

2 3-by-5-inch (7.6-by-12.7-cm)
    index cards
Scissors
Pen
Envelope

Cut the index cards in half so that you have 4 2½-by-3-inch (6.3-by-7.6-cm) cards. Write the following actions based on insect metamorphosis, one to a card.

Place all four cards (including the blank one) into the envelope for safekeeping until you are ready to create your *Insectigations!* game.

- A wasp is looking to lay its eggs on a larva. Roll any insect die. If you roll an insect with a land-based larva, go back to start.

- You finished your final molt. Roll the thorax die. If you are a grasshopper, jump ahead 3 spaces.

- A car just hit a squirrel. If a roll of any insect die shows you are a fly or beetle, take an extra turn.

After searching for insect eggs or attracting their parents, and watching the young grow and change, you now know what insects look like when they are immature and mature. But how did those flies find the meat in the spontaneous generation jar? Find out through the following sense-sational experiments and activities.

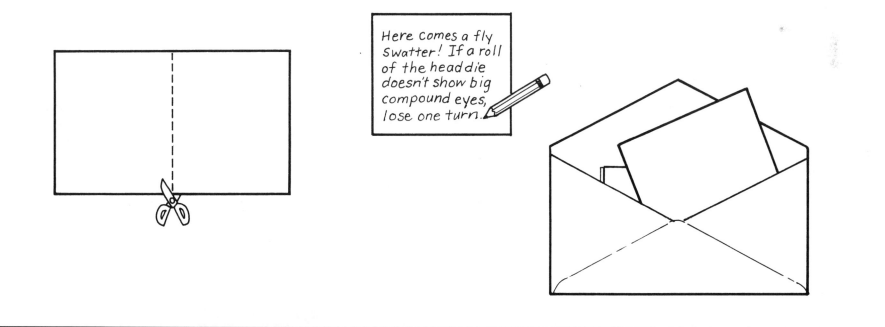

Here comes a fly swatter! If a roll of the head die doesn't show big compound eyes, lose one turn.

4

Sense-sational

The fly buzzing around the kitchen has landed near your sandwich. As it walks toward your plate, you slowly creep toward it, flyswatter raised overhead. Just as you swing the swatter down, it darts away. Then it comes back to buzz around your head before flying off. You wonder, how did the fly find your food, and how did it know you were about ready to swat it? Get ready to find out as you test how well you smell and if you see like a bee.

Vision

While some fleas are blind and must use their senses of smell and heat detection to find their food, some dragonflies have 23,000 lenses in each eye and can spot a mosquito flying near a pond. Just like with people, being able to see isn't everything, but it sure helps when you want to find food, escape enemies, and find each other!

Insects have two kinds of eyes, simple and compound. The simple eyes are called ocelli. Some larvae have up to six ocelli, while many adult insects have between one and three. You can usually find ocelli on an adult on the top of the head in-between the antennae. These eyes are sensitive to light but cannot see images. Ocelli help insects keep their balance and fly up, down, and around corners without going upside down or on their sides.

It is the compound eyes that see things. They are called compound eyes because each eye is made of between two and 23,000 lenses. Each lens sees a slightly different image and sends that information to eight special cells called photoreceptors (FŌ-tō-re-SEP-ters). These photoreceptors send the information to the brain, where all the images get put together to create a picture.

But most insects are near-sighted—their eyes only focus on things that are close by. Even then, the picture is fuzzy. With all those lenses, why does an insect's brain create a fuzzy picture? Although it has more lenses than we do, there are only 24,000 photoreceptors in the housefly's whole eye. There are around five million photoreceptors in just the middle part of a human's eye.

No problem—most insects don't need to see small details. What they really need to see is motion. Your two eyes can only look in one direction at a time. But insects with big eyes and a lot of lenses can see almost all the way around their bodies, which is why it is so hard to sneak up on them.

Wrong

Rob Harris

What a fly sees.

Brian G. Burton, Boston University

Real Entomologists

Although insects may see fuzzy pictures, they are very good at avoiding things (like your flyswatter). Engineers are using insect eyes as models for creating computer eyes that can be put in robotic planes. They want the planes to be able to fly without running into things.

Point of View

With two working eyes, you have two lenses. These two lenses are about 2.5 inches (6.25 cm) apart at the pupils. This small distance means that each eye sees things just a little bit differently. The difference is enough to give you *depth perception,* that is, visual clues as to how close or distant an object is, and how fast it is moving.

To see how this works, make your hand into the shape of an "o." Stretch your arm out, and with both eyes open, look through the o at something in the distance. Without moving your hand, close one eye. Is the target still visible? Now open that eye and close the other eye. Is the target still visible?

The eye that saw the target through your o is your dominant eye. Cover this eye and try to play catch with a soft ball. What happens?

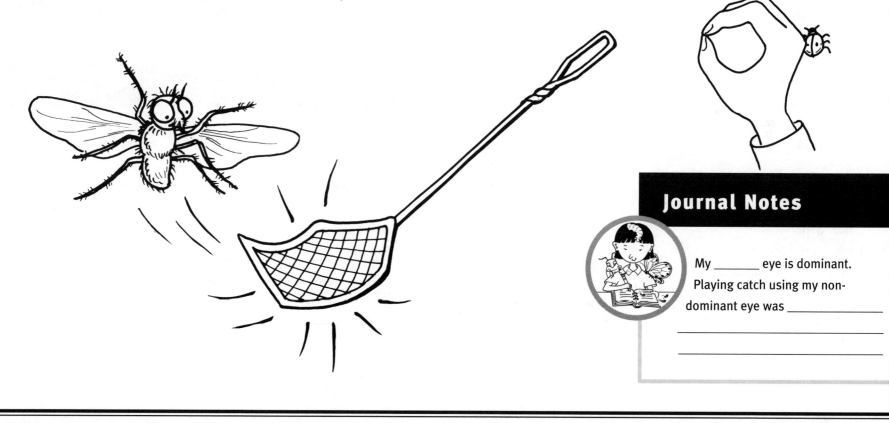

Journal Notes

My _____ eye is dominant. Playing catch using my non-dominant eye was _____

_____

_____

Colorblind Challenge

Not only do insects see fuzzy pictures, many are what we call colorblind. This doesn't mean they see everything in black and white. Colorblind means that some colors look the same as each other. In one form of colorblindness, violet, lavender, pink, and blue all appear as blue to the viewer. How the colors appear can also change depending on whether the viewer is in bright sunlight or in foggy conditions.

Materials

Scissors

Red, blue, green, yellow, pink, purple, and brown construction paper

A manila file folder or other lightweight cardboard

1 4-by-6-inch (10-by-15.25-cm) piece of green cellophane

Tape

Pen

Cut one 3-inch (7.5 cm) square of each color out of construction paper and put aside. Keeping the file folder folded, cut it in half. Then cut a 3-by-5-inch (7.6-by-12.7-cm) rectangle through both layers of one half. Open the folder, cover one of the rectangles with the green cellophane and tape it in place. Close the folder and tape the edges together to make a viewer.

1

File Folder

2

Shuffle the construction paper cards, then hold the colored viewer in front of your eyes and look at the cards one at a time.

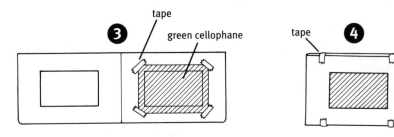

3 tape / green cellophane

4 tape

Use the pen to write down the color you see on the card. After you have looked at all the cards, lower the viewer.

Journal Notes

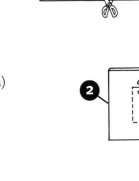

When I looked through the green viewer, this is what I saw:

Actual Color	What I Saw
Red	
Blue	
Green	
Yellow	
Pink	
Purple	
Brown	

Repeat the experiment outside on a bright sunny or foggy day, and with a viewer using red cellophane instead of green. Also look at the grass, leaves, and especially flowers!

Butterflies can see red, but honeybees can't, and they both can see yellow, blue, and even ultraviolet, which we can't see. Without color to confuse them, insects pay more attention to other clues, like shapes and movements.

Training Bees

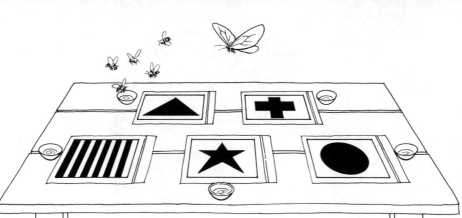

You can test the vision abilities of bees, butterflies, and other nectar eaters by providing food for them in this simple experiment.

Materials

5 plain index cards
Black marker
5 clear zippered plastic bags
5 shallow dishes

¾ cup (177 ml) hot water
¼ cup (59 ml) sugar
Spoon
Plain colored index cards

Draw the following shapes, one on each card: triangle, cross, stripes, star, and circle. Make sure you color the shapes in so they are solid, not just an outline. Find a large flat space like a picnic table or driveway in a sunny, calm area that won't be disturbed for several days. Put each card in a clear, zippered bag so that dew or a water spill won't hurt it. Place a shallow dish near each symbol. Pour plain water into four of the dishes. Pour the sugar into ¾ cup (177ml) very hot water (be sure to ask for an adult's help with this) and stir until it dissolves. Pour the sugar solution into the fifth dish. Watch the dishes for several days, until you are confident the insects know which bowl has sugar water. Change the order of cards and dishes, keeping the sugar water with the same pattern and watch what happens. Then keep the sugar water in the same place, but change the pattern that is near it. Finally, try the experiment again using plain colored cards instead of cards with symbols.

Make a Connection

To see if you are color-blind, visit www.toledo-bend.com/colorblind/Ishihara.html. This page has seven large circles. Each circle is filled with bubbles of different colors. One set of colored bubbles in each circle makes the shape of a number. Place your colored viewer over the circles. Does it affect your ability to see the numbers?

Journal Notes

How long did it take for bees or other insects to find the sugar water?
Were they confused when you changed the order of the dishes and cards?
Were they confused when you changed the pattern that was near the sugar water?
What happened when you used colored cards instead of patterned cards?
Did all insects (butterflies, flies, bees, beetles) react the same?

Make a Connection

To see what some patterns look like to a honeybee, visit http://cvs.anu.edu.au/andy/beye/beyehome.html. If you can imagine what it would look like if you pasted a large flower onto a basketball, then let some of the air out, you have a good idea of how a honeybee sees!

Some beekeepers rent out hives to farmers for crop pollination. If a bee tries to enter the wrong hive, guard bees will chase it out or even kill it. To help the bees find their own hives when they are in a new area, beekeepers can attach a simple shape, a colored patch, or a combination of the two near the entrance door.

Lightning bugs (also known as fireflies) are familiar beetles that light up the summer nights with their flickering flashes. It is the males who fly around flashing. They are looking for a female who is perched on a plant to flash back. The way lightning beetles tell each other apart is by the code they flash. Some do three short flashes in a row, others might do one short flash followed by a long flash as they fly up, making a "J." Success to a firefly means finding the same kind of beetle. This is easier than it sounds. Some types of fireflies copy the codes of others. But if the male lands near a female who is not the same kind as he is, she may eat him!

The next time you are out catching lightning beetles, challenge yourself to see if you can find a male (flying) and female (resting on a plant) of the same species. How good are you at deciphering their code?

Smell

Have you ever noticed how quickly flies find food? It doesn't matter if it is your picnic lunch in a park or an animal hit by a car, flies are often the first insect on the scene. How do they do it?

Because of their exoskeletons, insects have "noses" on the surface of their bodies. This helps make them more sensitive to smells. Most insects can detect smells with their antennae, but some, like flies and butterflies, use their feet!

Jean Henri Fabre was an entomologist interested in insect behavior. One summer, after watching a female peacock moth emerge from its cocoon, he put the large insect in a wire cage. That night, dozens of male peacock moths came flying in through open windows. He wondered how the male moths knew where the female moth was. To find out, he shaved a patch of fur off their abdomens so he could recognize returning moths. He clipped the antennae off some of the male moths. He turned off the lanterns. He also put the female in a new place each day for the next eight days. He put her in a closet. He put her in a drawer. He put her in a hatbox.

The only times no male moths came near her was when she was someplace where the air couldn't get out. Although the first female moth died before he found an answer, he didn't stop experimenting. After many more experiments, he concluded that some insects create their own smells (later called *pheromones*) to use in communication. People might not be able to smell the pheromones (FER-a-mōn), but male moths with their large, feathery antennae needed only a few parts per million to find the female.

Gross Entomology: *Maggots as Medicine*

Flies are very sensitive to the smell of meat. Many female flies like to lay their eggs on meat to provide food for their babies. During past wars when many people were wounded, it could take several days for all the injured soldiers to be found and taken to a doctor. Since the soldiers were lying outside, sometimes the doctors found maggots inside the wounds. After some time, the doctors noticed that the soldiers who had maggots in their wounds recovered faster than the soldiers who did not. They studied what was happening and discovered that the maggots only ate the dead flesh, helping to clean the wounds. Not only that, but the maggots produced a chemical called allantoin, which helped the wounds heal faster. Look at the ingredients lists of hand and suntan lotions, antiperspirants and deodorants, toothpastes, and soaps. Do you have any allantoin in your house?

Concentration

When female insects release pheromones (a chemical smell) to attract a mate, the antennae on the males often have more branches to help them pick up the scent. The male emperor moth has the most acute sense of smell in the animal kingdom. It can detect one molecule of pheromone from 6.8 miles away. How good are your senses of smell and taste?

Materials

10 clear cups
Pen or marker
Red juice
Spoon
Water

Number the clear cups 1 through 10. Put ten spoonfuls of juice in cup #1. Put nine spoonfuls of water in cups #2 through #10. Take one spoonful of juice from cup #1 and put it in cup

#2. Mix it well. Take one spoonful of liquid from cup #2 and put it in cup #3. After mixing it well, take one spoonful of liquid from cup #3 and put it in cup #4. Repeat this pattern until you have taken one spoonful of liquid from #9 and added it to #10.

Cup #1 has all juice. In cup #2, you have 1 part of juice in 10 parts of liquid. As you mix the juice with water, you are diluting it, having less and less in each next cup. By the time you get to cup #6, you have only one part of juice in one million parts of water. In cup #10, you have one part juice in one billion parts of water.

Real Entomologists

If forest trees start to look bare in the middle of summer, scientists try to figure out why. To see if the problem is caused by too many gypsy moth caterpillars eating the green leaves, scientists use pheromones to lure male gypsy moths into traps. Biologists count how many male moths they catch, then use that number to estimate how many moths are in the area. If they decide there are too many moths, they might consider using an insect spray to try to kill them.

The inside of this trap is coated with sticky papers and gypsy moth pheromone.

Journal Notes

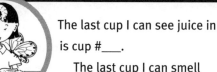

The last cup I can see juice in is cup #___.
The last cup I can smell the juice in is cup # ___.
The last cup I can taste the juice in is cup # ___.

If you were an insect sensitive to juice, you might be able to still taste or smell it in cups #8 (100 parts per billion) and #9 (10 parts per billion).

Dinner Detour

Materials

Piece of cake, cookie, or sugary
   doughnut
Leaves
Sticks
Thin strips of paper
Watch or clock

Do ants living near you use
their sense of sight or their sense
of smell to find their way? Set a
piece of cake, cookie, or sugary
doughnut on the ground about
five feet away from an active
anthill. Place several obstacles like
leaves, sticks, and thin strips of
paper between the food and the
anthill. Record the time in your
journal, then find a comfortable
place where you can watch what
happens.

Once it looks like all the ants
are following the same trail,
move some of the obstacles
around. If their trail takes
them over a piece of paper,
turn the paper so it faces a different way. Move a stick so a different part of it is over the trail.
Remove leaves or turn them
upside down. From the
changes you make, can you
tell if the ants are using
smell or vision as clues on
their trails? Record what
happens in your journal.

Army ants are blind and must
use their sense of smell to get
around, while carpenter ants use
both sight and smell. There are
more than 550 species of ants in
North America, so if you look
around, you will probably find
more than one type of ant living
near you. Make a sketch of each
ant type in your journal, noting
its size and color. Repeat your
experiment on as many different
types of ants as you can find.

Journal Notes

After I moved

_____,

the ants had/had no trouble
finding their food.

Journal Notes

Start time:
   It took _____ minutes for the
first ant to find the food.
   It took _____ minutes for more ants
to bring back others.
   I think the ants are using _____
to find their way.

Action Cards

Materials

Scissors
2 3-by-5-inch (7.6-by-12.7-cm)
   index cards
Pen
Envelope

Cut the index cards in half so that you have 4 2½-by-3-inch (6.3-by-7.6-cm) cards. Copy the following actions based on insect senses, one to a card. Place all four cards (including the blank one) into the envelope for safekeeping until you are ready to create your *Insectigations!* game.

- Mmmm. If a roll of the head die shows you have the feathery antennae you need to smell the rotting fruit near the tree, take an extra turn.
- A human has moved your home. If a roll of the head die shows you have bee eyes, go ahead 4 spaces.
- Scientists are testing a new pheromone trap. Roll the head die. If you have short antennae, you can't sense the smell and fly free. All others lose a turn.

So insects can communicate through their sense of smell. Is there any other way for them to talk? Of course there is! Get ready for a buzzy, buggy time!

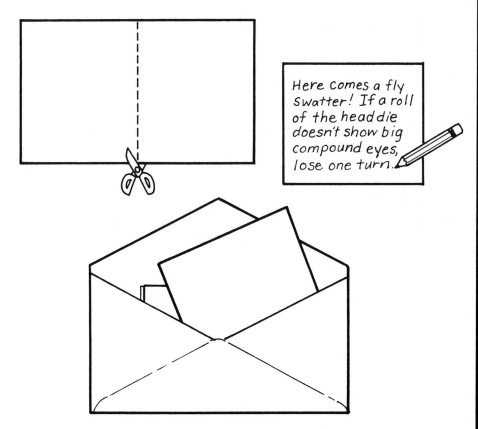

Here comes a fly swatter! If a roll of the head die doesn't show big compound eyes, lose one turn.

5

Can We Talk?

Although they don't speak with words we recognize, insects communicate in some pretty amazing ways. From their antennae to their toes, insects use the various parts of their bodies to keep in touch. A female toci-toci beetle can use her antennae to listen to the tapping made by a male more than three miles away. Grasshoppers rub their legs together to make chirping sounds. Male and female mosquitoes flap their wings at different speeds, giving them an easy way to tell each other apart.

When male cicadas start their abdominal chorus, they can drown out sounds of a nearby highway. You might say that insects have a way without words! Find out how as you watch sound waves at work, listen in on insect sounds, and create your own buzzing bug.

Sounds of Summer

You are sitting outside on a warm day with a glass of lemonade in your hand, and then you hear it. An insect is coming to check you out. Is it a bee or a

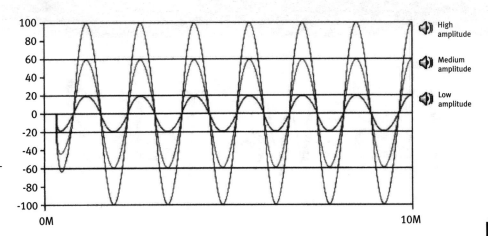

mosquito? A fly or a wasp? A cicada or a katydid? How can you tell without even looking? By listening! These insects may not be intentionally notifying you of their arrival, but their sounds are like fingerprints for the ear.

What is sound? For a long time, scientists considered sound to be only those vibrations that traveled through the air and activated our sense of hearing. But as they studied other animals such as dolphins, whales, and elephants, scientists became convinced that animals

were sending and receiving signals through water, wood, and even the earth itself. So the definition of sound was expanded to include any vibration of air, liquids, or solids.

No matter who makes the vibration or what it is traveling through, sound moves in waves. These waves can be measured in several ways. The height of these waves is called the *amplitude*. The amplitude gives information about the volume of a sound. A large or high wave produces a louder sound than a small or short wave.

The measurement of the wavelength is called the *frequency*. Waves that are short from front to back (fast) are said to have a high frequency and a high pitch sound. The wavelength of A above middle C is about 2.6 feet (.8 m), while the wavelength of A below middle C is about 5.1 feet (1.5 m).

Make a Connection

Not sure if you have ever heard a cicada or cricket? Go to www.naturesongs. com and listen in. Cicadas make a clicking, buzzing sound that pulses like an emergency siren. Crickets create a cheery chirp that is a bit like the low-battery signal in a smoke detector.

Sounds Abound

Infrasonic sounds are those that are too low for humans to hear. Elephants use their nasal passages to create low, rumbling, infrasonic sounds that can travel nearly seven miles. *Ultrasonic* sounds are those that are too high for humans to hear. They are often used in medicine for functions ranging from taking pictures of internal organs (ultrasounds) to smashing kidney stones. *Supersonic* sounds are those that deal with solid bodies that exceed the speed of sound, such as when a supersonic jet breaks the sound barrier and you hear a loud BOOM!

Wing Waves

It's late at night and both an Asian vampire moth and a female mosquito are in your room, looking for a meal of blood. Which one are you going to hear and have a chance to swat before you become dinner?

Materials

A wooden yardstick (meter stick)
A table

Place the stick on the table with 2 inches (5 cm) hanging over the edge. Hold the remaining length of stick firmly on the table with one hand. Watch and listen to what happens as you push the thumb on your free hand down and off the hanging edge. Increase the part of the stick that hangs over the edge to 4 inches (10 cm) and repeat the experiment. Continue the activity increasing the part that hangs over the edge by 2 inches (5 cm) each time until you have only 2 inches (5 cm) remaining on the table.

As the hanging edge gets longer, does the sound get higher or lower?

Does the hanging piece move faster or slower?

Does the sound get louder or softer?

The 2-inch (5-cm) piece of stick doesn't have much length to move, making its wavelength short, giving it a high frequency and a high-pitched sound. The 34-inch (95 cm) piece has a greater length to travel, producing a longer, slower sound wave with a lower pitch. What this means is that a mosquito with a wingspan of around one-half inch (1.3 cm) produces a high-pitched whine, while you never hear the vampire moths that have wingspans several inches (or centimeters) wide.

Notable Insects

Depending upon the size of an insect, the size of its wings, how warm it is, and what it is trying to do, it will flap its wings at different speeds. If you were to listen to insects while playing the piano, you could match their sounds with these piano notes.

Crickets, katydids, and cicadas are definitely the stars of an insect orchestra, but that may be because of where they live—above ground and out in the open. Most of your hearing happens when vibrations in the air reach your eardrums. Insects living inside wood or underwater could be singing a symphony, and you would never know it.

Do You Hear What I Hear?

Just under the bark of a dead or dying tree, adult click beetles, stag beetle larvae, and termites all stake out a dinner claim as they gnaw through the decaying wood. After the sounds of their chewing alert a woodpecker to their location, they may beat their heads against the walls of their tunnels and nests to warn others of the approaching attack. Listen carefully as you gently scratch the top of a wooden table. Lay one ear on the table and scratch again. Notice any difference? Can you hear anything if you put your ear against a dead tree?

When you make a sound through air vibrations, the air scatters the sound in all directions. When you direct your sound efforts through a solid, such as wood, the vibrations are more contained, and therefore are stronger (or louder). So an

Measuring Sounds

Two common words used when scientists are talking about sounds are hertz and decibels. *Hertz* (abbreviated Hz) is the measurement of the frequency, or how many sound waves pass a given point in one second. One kilohertz (kHz) is 1,000 cycles per second; 1 megahertz (MHz) is 1 million cycles per second. Humans can hear sound frequencies from about 20 Hz to about 20 kHz. You don't hear your own heartbeat because it beats too slowly, and you can't hear a high-pitched dog whistle because it produces a sound at 30 kHz or more.

Decibels are the measurement of sound energy and intensity, which is related to loudness. Zero (0) is the softest sound that humans can hear. Sounds louder than 85 decibels can cause hearing damage if you are exposed to them for too long.

As an example of the difference between the two terms, think of a cicada. Male cicadas produce a song that creates a sound wave measuring 390 Hz, which is about the same pitch you hear for the word "star" when you sing *Twinkle, Twinkle, Little Star* (G above middle C on the piano). Their song is one of the loudest noises made by an animal, registering up to 112 decibels, which is about the same loudness as a rock concert or leaf blower.

Common Insects Measured Sound Wave Rates (c/s = cycles per second) Closest Piano Note Equivalents	Butterfly	Dragonfly	Bumblebee	Tired Bee	Housefly	Active Bee	Mosquito	No-see-um midge
	8–20 c/s	40 c/s	117 c/s	326 c/s	345 c/s	435 c/s	587 c/s	1050 c/s
	too low to hear	the third E below middle C	the second A below middle C	E above middle C	F above middle C	A above middle C	D one octave above middle C	C two octaves above middle C

animal communicating through wood has to use less effort than one that is communicating through air.

Water Words

When you are near water, frogs and ducks might make so much noise that you can't hear anything else. But if you watch and listen carefully, you might witness aquatic insects using their own water words. To attract a mate, the male backswimmer makes a very loud noise by rubbing his front legs together or against his beak. You can hear him 130 feet (40 m) away under water. Whirligig beetles are like bats. They use echolocation to find their food. The beetles feed on insects that fall into the water, detecting them by the ripples they make.

Insect Ears

You may know that some insects use their antennae to sense sound, but have you ever looked for an insect's ears? What do

Night Life

During the quiet hours of late night, it is much easier to hear sounds that are usually missed during the day. Night is also a time of hidden insect activity. Years ago, as people would sit up at night with a sick relative or friend, they would sometimes hear a tap-tap-tap sound coming from within the walls of the house. Since medicine and doctors were hard to come by, many times the sick person died. People started to believe that when they heard tapping noises at night, someone was about to die. When they discovered that the sound was made by a wood-eating beetle living in the timbers of their house, banging its head on its tunnels to attract a mate, they named the insect "the death-watch beetle."

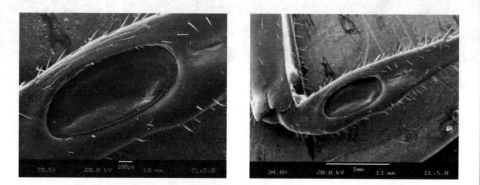

These scanning electron micrographs produce highly magnified views of a katydid's leg, showing its ear. Anna Price, Department of Biology, Wake Forest University

insects' ears look like, and where are they located? Most insects' ears are simply a thin membrane called a tymbal, stretched over a very small hole, so they look like the top of a drum. But you won't see an insect's ears on the side of its head. You would need to use a powerful magnifier and look on a green lacewing's wings, on the inside of a katydid's or cricket's knees, or on the side of a short-horned grasshopper's body at the base of its abdomen!

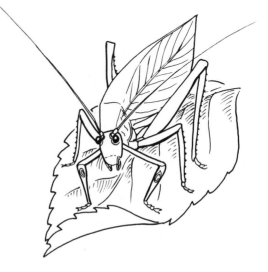

When a tiger moth hears the high-pitched clicks of a bat headed its way, it responds by dropping like a stone while making clicks of its own, trying to jam the bat's radar.

Materials

Scissors
1 large balloon
Short stiff tube, such as a
    plastic soda bottle with
    both ends cut off
Rubber bands
Rice or cereal, several grains

Cut the balloon in half around the circumference, then stretch a piece over each end of the tube and secure the pieces with rubber bands. Hold the tube upright and place a few grains of rice or cereal on top. Gently tap the lower balloon membrane and watch what happens.

Journal Notes

When I tap the lower balloon membrane, this is what happens:

_____

When you tap the balloon, you are making it vibrate. The vibrations are transferred to the air inside the tube, and then to the balloon on top, making it vibrate and the grains jump.

Buzzing Bug

Children in Africa sometimes catch the giant Goliath beetle, tie one end of string to one of its legs, and the other end to a stick. Then, as the beetle flies overhead in a circle, it makes a loud buzzing noise. You can make a vibration sensation by creating your own buzzing bug.

Materials

1 18-inch (45-cm) piece
   of string
Popsicle/craft stick
Scissors
Stiff paper
Markers
Glue
Stapler
1 1-inch (2.5-cm) diameter
   foam ball
Wide rubber band

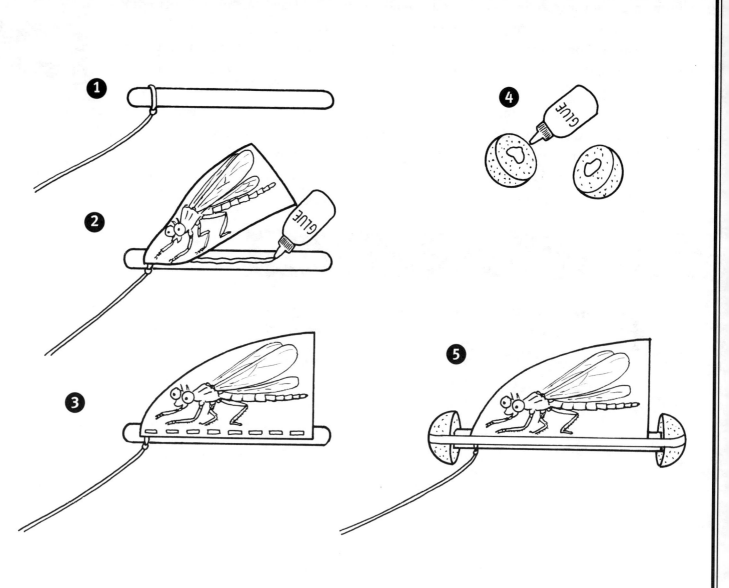

Tie one end of the string around one end of the craft stick. Cut the piece of paper so that one edge is straight and slightly smaller than the Popsicle stick. Draw a flying insect on both sides of the paper. Glue the straight edge of the paper to the middle of the stick, covering the string. Staple the paper and the string to the stick. Cut the foam ball in half. Dab glue on each flat side. Place one half on each end of the stick. Stretch the rubber band around the stick and craft ball ends. After the glue dries, go outside and swing the buzzer over your head.

Some insects use body parts other than wings to make sounds. To mimic the chirp of crickets, grasshoppers, and katy-dids rubbing their legs or wings together, rub a stick across the teeth of a comb. Press the button on a baby food jar lid in and out to copy a cicada clicking its abdomen. To sound like the vibrating spiracles of the Madagascar hissing cock-roach, stretch the neck of an inflated balloon apart as you slowly let the air escape.

Bees Buzz Around the World

While many English-speaking people say that bees buzz, other languages have other words for it. In Spain, bees are said to *zumbar*, in Germany they *summen*, in Israel they *zimzum,* and they *brzecza* in Poland.

Journal Notes

What is making the sound? How can I change the sound? The foam ball pieces hold the rubber band away from the craft stick, giving it room to vibrate as it moves through the air. Your swinging speed plus the width and length of the rubber band affect how quickly it can vibrate, which determines the sound it makes.

Insect Amplifier

Some insects are very hard to hear. An *amplifier* is something that makes a sound louder. Use this simple amplifier to help you hear the sound an insect makes.

Materials
Sound-producing insect
1 paper cup
Piece of waxed paper large
    enough to cover top of cup
Rubber band
Timer

Catch an insect that makes an audible sound. (Don't select a stinging insect for this experiment.) Carefully transfer the insect to a paper cup. Place the waxed paper over the mouth of the cup, then use the rubber band to keep it in place. Put the cup up to your ear and listen. To slow down an insect and change its sound, put the cup, with the insect in it, into a refrigerator for up to 10 minutes. But don't forget to take it out! Set the timer for 10 minutes to help you remember. After you're finished listening, be sure to set your singer free.

Sometimes, it is better not to be heard. When male crickets are chirping trying to attract a mate, their calls can also attract tachinid flies. These flies are parasites. They lay their eggs inside the cricket. When the larvae hatch out of the eggs inside of the cricket, the cricket dies.

You might be surprised by how loud an insect can sound.

Dig This

Another simple amplifier is a cone shape (such as a megaphone). Cones amplify by directing sound waves toward their targets, rather than letting them scatter in all directions. The male mole cricket digs his burrow in the shape of a double megaphone. Then he sits behind it and "sings" his song. The double megaphone is so effective that a person can hear his song from almost a quarter mile away.

Journal Notes

This is the kind of insect I put in the cup: _____

_____

The insect sounded like this:

_____

After I chilled the insect in the cup, this is what it sounded like:

_____

_____

This works on the same principle as the model ear, only this time the insect makes the air in the enclosed chamber vibrate, which in turn makes the waxed paper vibrate. By containing these vibrations to a small space, the effect of the vibrations is increased, or amplified. You can use the cup without the waxed paper to amplify the insect sounds coming from a dead tree. Place the open end of the cup against the tree and your ear on the bottom of the cup.

Sound Off Sentry

People have learned to use insect sounds to their advantage. In Japan, people keep crickets in special cages. As long as everything is still and quiet, the cricket chirps in its cage. But if a human or large animal comes near, the cricket stops chirping. This sudden quiet warns the cricket's owner that somebody is nearby. So, think of a cricket as a reverse watchdog!

Materials

Egg cartons
Paper towels
Aquarium or hamster cage with a tight-fitting screen lid
Crickets
Damp sponge
Small jar lid
Fruit and vegetable pieces (lettuce, apples, etc.)

Place the egg cartons and crumpled paper towels in the bottom of the aquarium to give crickets a place to hide. Either catch some crickets or buy them at a pet store. Put a piece of damp sponge on a small jar lid for water. Every day, place some lettuce leaves, apple slices or other fruit and vegetable pieces in the aquarium cage and rewet the sponge. Remove the uneaten pieces of food every day so that you don't start a fly farm as well. Listen to the crickets at different times of the day and night.

Journal Notes

What time are the crickets noisiest?

How long are the crickets quiet after I enter the room?

Do the crickets change their chirping speed as the weather changes?

You can use crickets as watchdogs, and you can also use them as a simple thermometer.

Although snowy tree crickets usually produce the most accurate results, you can try this experiment with any cricket you hear. Simply count the number of chirps you hear in 15 seconds and add 37. The result is approximately the temperature in degrees Fahrenheit. For degrees Celsius, count the number of chirps in 15 seconds, divide by 2 and add 6.

Action Cards

Materials

2 3-by-5-inch (7.6-by-12.7-cm)
   index cards
Scissors
Pen
Envelope

Cut the index cards in half so that you have 4 2½-by-3-inch (6.3-by-7.6-cm) cards. Copy the following actions based on insect sounds, one to a card. Place all four cards (including the blank one) into the envelope for safekeeping until you are ready to create your *Insectigations!* game.

- You are trying to sneak across the basement. If a roll of the thorax die shows you are a noisemaker, lose one turn.

- A bat is looking for dinner. If a roll of the thorax die shows you are a flying insect, go back to start.

- You are looking for a mate. If a roll of the thorax die shows you are a noisemaker, take an extra turn.

Whether or not you have learned to speak fluent cricket, or your bug buzzer creates the same pitch as a bee, the tips and tricks in chapter 6 will help you find insects wherever and whenever you want to look.

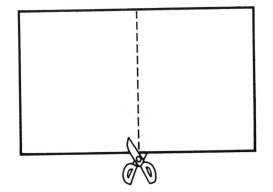

Here comes a fly swatter! If a roll of the head die doesn't show big compound eyes, lose one turn.

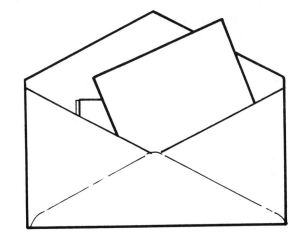

6

Finders

Fossils show us that insects were living on Earth even before the dinosaurs. In the millions of years insects have been around, our world has changed a lot. There have been floods, ice ages, volcanic eruptions, and meteor crashes. Although these events killed most of the insects and other animals that existed at these times, enough insects survived to continue reproducing. As the world changed, so did the insects. Their bodies and habits adapted to the different environments, so that now, insects can be found almost everywhere. Tiny non-biting, mosquito-looking midges can be found in Antarctica. On ocean coasts, the seashore spring-tail hides in air-filled pockets under rocks at high tide, then looks like a speck of dirt as it springs along the shore looking for plant litter to eat when the water has receded. Fleas find your pets irresistible, moths like your clothes, and cockroaches hide in your basement.

In order to reduce competition for food and other necessities, insects have become active at various times: day, night, winter, spring, summer, or fall. Although it is easiest to find the greatest variety of insects outside at dusk on a summer evening, you can look for fuzzy white mealybugs attached to the underside of the leaves of your houseplants anytime. Snow fleas can be found at the base of trees on a winter day, while cicadas sing on hot summer evenings.

With so many out there, insects should be easy to find—right? Maybe. Maybe not! Treehoppers can look like thorns. Walking sticks—as their name suggests—look like sticks. The South American hawk caterpillar looks like a snake, and *Salvodora* species of caterpillars look like bird poop!

If insects are so well camouflaged, then how can you watch, catch, or collect them? The activities in this chapter give you tips and tricks to finding a large variety and number of insects.

Sweep Net

You can look for insects one at a time, but they are masters at hiding and escaping. An easier way to catch a wide variety and high number of insects is to use a sweep net.

Materials

Pliers

Wire coat hanger

Wire cutter

Scissors

Old pillowcase (with no holes)

Old broomstick (or thick dowel rod)

Duct tape

Metal hose clamp, optional (sold in hardware or automotive stores)

Screwdriver

Looking jar

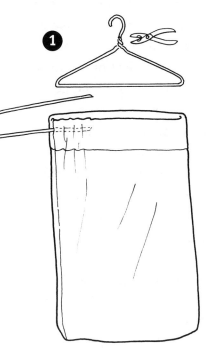

Ask an adult to help you use the pliers to untwist the coat hanger and form an open loop. Use the wire cutters to snip off the hook, saving it for the activity Fly-Tying a Big Bug (on page 98). Cut a small slit in the hem at the mouth of the pillowcase. Thread the coat hanger through the hem. Place one end of the coat hanger now threaded through the pillowcase on each side of the broomstick. Wrap the wire and broomstick with duct tape. For extra holding power, slip a circular, metal hose clamp over the duct tape and coat hanger, then tighten its screw using a screwdriver.

Hold the sweep net a few inches off the ground as you walk through a grassy area.

To use a sweep net, go to an area with grass. One of the best places to find insects is at the top of the tallest hill in an area. Many male butterflies, moths, and other insects head up high to make it easier for females to find them, but any weedy field or even your backyard is fine. Hold the net end a few inches above the ground. Walk forward and swivel the net opening from side to side as you sweep through the grass, knocking insects off the plants and into your net. After about 20 steps, lift the net up and let any stinging insects fly free. Grab the net around the middle so that no other insects can escape, then gently shake your catch as you move your hand down the bag. When your hand is only about 3 inches (7 to 8 cm) from the bottom, move the net close to the mouth of your looking jar. Carefully open your net-filled hand while you use your free hand to gently turn the pillowcase inside out as you transfer the insects into the looking jar. Shake any clinging insects off the net and then remove the net with one hand while you put the lid on the jar with the other hand.

If you follow the same instructions using sheer curtains instead of a pillowcase, you will make an aerial net. Aerial nets are more delicate, so you shouldn't sweep the grass with them. You can use an aerial net to catch an insect such as a butterfly, moth, or dragonfly as it is flying, or wait until an insect has landed, then gently drop the net over it and surround it.

Insect Trap

What do a monarch butterfly, box elder bug, ladybird beetle, hunting safety vest, construction cone, and stop sign have in common? They all use bright red or orange colors to send a warning message. What are they saying? Usually it is "Hey! Be careful around me!" Most insects that have noticeable red or orange markings also taste pretty bad and can make predators gag. So an animal might try to eat a red one once, then leave all other red ones alone!

Sweep nets work well for insects that are crawling on plant leaves and stems. But ants, roaches, and many beetles spend much of their time on the ground. A pit trap is a better way to catch these insects.

Materials

Scissors
1 2-liter bottle
Bait (raw meat the size of a meatball)
Small garden trowel
Four small, flat rocks
Board that is about 5 inches (13 cm) square

Cut off the top third of the bottle, making a funnel shape. Place the bait in the bottom piece of the bottle. Nest the funnel piece top upside down inside the bottle bottom. Use the trowel to dig a hole deep enough so that the top of the bottle will be even with the ground. (Check with an adult before digging.) The slick sides and funnel will keep many of the creatures that fall into the trap stuck inside. Place the rocks around the edge of the bottle, and place the board on top of the rocks. This will leave enough room for insects to investigate the smell, but keep rain and heavy dew out of the trap. Check on the trap every morning and again every evening. Do you trap more insects during the day or night?

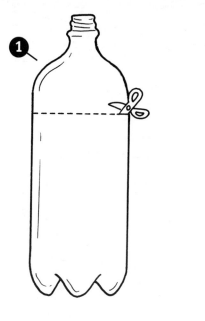

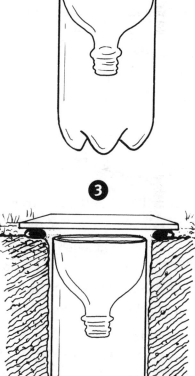

Leaf Litter Shaker

Springtails, scavenger beetles, jumping ground bugs, and other arthropods eat dead leaves and plants. Unless you put a trap right under them, you might not find these decomposers. To find them, you need to shake them out.

Materials

Plastic ice cream tub with lid
Thick rag
Pencil
Dead leaves
Light-colored sheet

Place the lid of the ice cream tub on the thick rag. Use the pencil to punch large holes in the lid. Fill the tub with clumps of dead leaves that are brown and crumbly, then put the lid on tightly. Hold the tub upside down over a light-colored sheet and shake it. In your journal, record which insects fall onto the sheet, sketch the different types, and include a total count.

Berlese's Itty-Bitty Bugs

Antonio Berlese was an Italian entomologist who studied very small insects and mites that spend most of their time in the soil. Although thousands of these tiny animals can live in just a shovelful of soil, it is hard to spy and catch them. Instead of looking in the soil for them, Berlese figured out how to get them to leave the soil. He placed a small screen near the bottom of a funnel. He put some soil in the funnel, and put the funnel in a tall jar that had alcohol in the bottom. He finished by putting some hot water around the funnel. As the soil warmed up and dried out, the small animals moved farther and farther down, until they fell out of the bottom of the funnel and into the jar. He shared his invention with other entomologists. Many years later, instead of using hot water, a scientist named Tullgren hung a lightbulb over the funnel. Today students and scientists all over the world use the Berlese-Tullgren funnel to see what animals are living in the soil.

Cockroach Catcher

Providing water is a great way to attract many insects. A cockroach can live for about a month without food, but for only about one week without water. Place a damp rag on the floor in your garage. (Check with an adult first.) Check under the rag early in the morning to see if a roach or any other insect is hiding underneath it.

Insect Rain

ere's another way to collect insects. In this collection activity you may find it raining insects.

Materials
Umbrella
Strong stick
Looking jar

Katydids and cicadas spend a great deal of time in trees. To catch them, open the umbrella and place it upside down under a tree or bush. Take a strong stick and hit a large branch of the tree or bush several times to knock insects off the branch and into the umbrella. Gently tap the sides of the umbrella to shake the insects down to the center, then scoop them into your looking jar.

You're on a Roll!

Here's another collection technique to find insects that are underfoot.

Materials

Large rocks, rotting logs, or
  boards (outside)
Crayon
Plain paper

Some insects spend most of their lives just out of sight. Carefully roll over large rocks, boards, and rotting logs to look for crickets, carpenter ants, bark beetles, wood roaches, termites, crickets, and their arthropod cousins, the millipedes, centipedes, and pillbugs.

In addition to finding insects, you might notice tunnels under the bark on a rotting log. These are created by bark beetles, with each type of beetle creating a unique tunnel pattern. Some entomologists can tell which beetles are around just by look-

ing at the tunnels. To save these patterns in your journal, peel the paper wrapping off of a crayon. Place a piece of plain paper over the bark beetle tunnel, then rub

the long, flat side of the crayon over the paper. The tunnels will appear as a lighter area on your colored paper, preserving evidence of your insect finds.

Carefully put the rocks, boards, and logs back in their original positions before you leave the area.

Bug Bait

Moths, stag beetles, caddisflies, and other insects that are active at night often use their sense of smell to find their food. Mix up a batch of bug bait to use on a warm summer night, and you will see insects that might otherwise escape your notice.

Materials

1 cup (240 ml) fruit juice
Large bowl with lid
Spoon
2 very ripe bananas
¼ cup (59 ml) sugar,
    honey, or molasses
Paintbrush
Flashlight
Sweep net
Looking jar

Leave the fruit juice on your kitchen counter in a covered bowl. After two days, open the lid and use the spoon to mash

Gross Entomology: *Pantry Pests*

Another place to look for insects is in the food you eat. Food would be too expensive to grow, harvest, and process if everyone had to get out all insect pieces and parts. Considering the fact that in many countries, people eat insects on purpose, it seems a bit silly to worry about a few ant antennae or beetle wings that might find their way into your mouth. But to make sure what you eat is safe, there are standards of how many insects or pieces of insects are allowed in different types of food. The U.S. Food and Drug Administration considers food safe even with the following amounts of insect parts:

Flour: Up to 75 insect fragments in about 2 cups (50 g)

Canned citrus juice: Five or more fruit fly eggs or other fly eggs in about 1 cup (250 ml)

Peanut butter: An average of 30 insect fragments in a little less than ½ cup (100 g)

Ground cinnamon: An average of 400 or more insect fragments per ⅓ cup (50 g)

the two very ripe bananas into the juice. Stir in the sugar, honey, or molasses. Since this recipe can attract a lot of insects, ask an adult which tree, fence post, or utility pole near your house would be the best place to paint the bug bait. Go outside before dark and use the paintbrush to paint the mixture on the chosen site. Wash the brush thoroughly so you can use it later to catch some of the insects. About an hour after dark, use a flashlight to check and see if any night prowling insects have found your sugar stash. You can use your sweep net to catch the flying ones, and the paintbrush to gently brush the crawling insects into your looking jar.

Make a Connection

If you want to eat insects on purpose, get some recipes that use insects at www.ent.iastate.edu/misc/insectsasfood.html.

White Light

While they are out looking for food, a mate, or trying to avoid bats, June bugs, luna moths, mayflies, and many other insects get together around lights at night. You can use this to your advantage as a way to catch even more insects.

Materials

String, rope, or clothesline
White sheet
Light source (porch light, flash-
light, lantern)
Newspaper
Looking jar

On a calm evening, string a rope between two trees or use a clothesline. Hang the white sheet over the rope or line. Turn on a light, lantern, or flashlight on one side of the sheet. Come back about two hours later to see how many different insects have landed on the sheet to be near the light. Place newspaper under the sheet and gently tap the sheet, making some of the insects fall onto the paper below. If you work quickly, you can tilt the paper and slide the insects into your looking jar so you can get a closer look.

Walking on Water

Water World

If you only look on land, you will miss seeing some very special insects. Aquatic insects have developed amazing adaptations to help them survive. Whirligig beetles have two pairs of eyes so they can see both above and below water at the same time. Diving beetles are scuba divers, rising to the surface to get a bubble of air under their shells so they can stay underwater longer. Dragonfly nymphs jet through the water by releasing a powerful squirt of water through their abdomens. And don't forget to take a second look at those skinny sticks moving across the top of the pond to see if they are really water striders walking on top of the water.

How do water striders and fishing spiders move across the top of the water without falling in? The shape of the animal and the attraction of water molecules to each other both play a part in keeping water walkers from getting wet feet.

Materials

Thin writing paper
Pencil
Scissors
Large-mouthed clear cup
Plate or pie pan
Water
Box of paper clips
Watch

Lay the piece of paper over the pattern of the water strider, trace the pattern onto the paper with your pencil, and cut the pattern out. Bend the feet along the lines so the strider can stand up, and put it to one side. Place

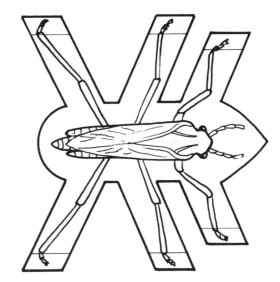

the clear cup on the plate or pie pan and fill it up to the very top with water. Count how many paper clips you can carefully slip into the water one at a time, making sure your fingers don't touch the water. Once the water is higher than the rim of the cup, carefully place the paper strider onto the water and use the watch to record how long it stays on top.

Journal Notes

I put _____ paper clips into the full glass of water.

When I put the paper strider on top of the water, this is what happened:

_____

This is how long the water strider floated on top of the water:

_____

Water molecules like to stick close to each other, showing a force called *cohesion* (co-HĒ-shun). Where the water molecules meet the air, their cohesion creates surface tension. This surface tension creates a thin skin on the water. This skin on the water is strong enough to support lightweight objects.

Animals that walk on water spread their weight over a large area so they won't break through the water's skin. Your paper strider should have remained on top until water soaked through its feet, causing it to become heavier and sink.

For a long time, scientists have known how water boatmen, backswimmers, and whirligig beetles use their oar-like legs to move across the water. What they didn't know was how the long-legged water strider, which walks on top of the water, moves forward. Two graduate students from the Massachusetts Institute of Technology decided to find out. After carefully studying water striders in action, it appeared to them that the striders were using their front and back legs for support, and their middle legs as oars. To test their theory, they created a robotic water strider using a 7-Up can, stainless steel wire legs, and a rubber band–powered pulley. They put the robot in dyed water and filmed the result. Sure enough, when the middle legs hit the water, they create tiny vortices (like miniature, underwater tornadoes) that move the water strider forward.

Water We Looking For?

Unless you plan on submerging yourself in a pond to see insects that have amazing aquatic adaptations, you'll have to catch the insects instead. While water striders and whirligigs are easy to find on the surface of a pond or stream, dragonfly nymphs, diving beetles, and many other insects hide under rocks, in the mud, or on the plants underwater.

Materials

Kitchen strainer with screen bottom

Small-screened aquarium net

Clear cup

Shallow dish with a white bottom

Magnifying lens

You can wait until you see an aquatic insect, then make a big splash trying to catch it, or, like the sweep net, you can catch a large number and variety of insects by simply scooping through the water with the strainer or net. Visit a shallow pond or stream in your area. (Check with an adult first.) Pull the net across the top of the water, then past plants, and through the mud. If you get too much mud, use the cup to pour pond water through the net. After most of the mud is gone, see which insects you have caught. If you are looking in a stream, pick some rocks from the stream bottom and see if anything is hanging on to them. To get a better look, put the insects and some water in the white-bottomed dish and use your magnifying lens. Since water is a natural magnifier, you can also fill your clear cup with water and insects and watch them in action. Of course, you might also see some non-insect creatures including tadpoles, shrimp-like scuds, leeches, worms, crayfish, and spiders, too.

Visit a pond throughout the year to catch an amazing variety of aquatic insects.

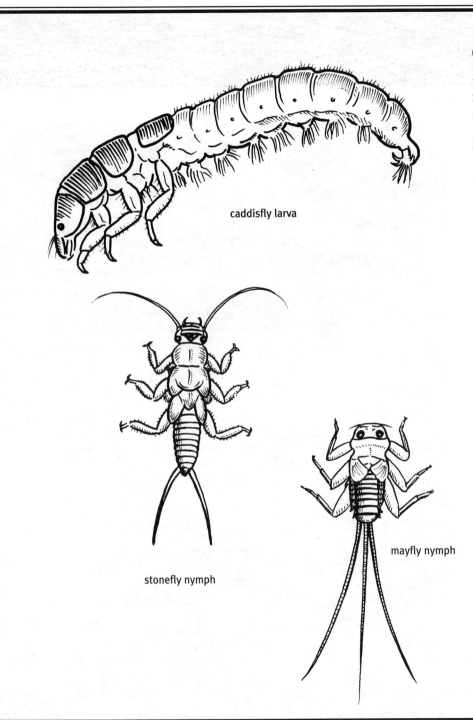

caddisfly larva

stonefly nymph

mayfly nymph

mayfly nymph

Clean Water Monitors

Next to air, water is probably the most essential item for living things. People need clean (not polluted) water for drinking, cleaning, cooking, playing, fishing, growing foods, and many other activities. One way water experts determine the quality of water in a stream is by looking for aquatic nymphs and larvae of insects. The rule of thumb is that the less polluted the water is, the greater the variety and number of species you will find in it.

As a quick way to determine the quality of stream water, monitors can look for immature insects that are very sensitive to pollution. They go to where the water is moving fast and find three hand-sized rocks that are not buried under mud or other rocks. They pick up the rocks and turn them over, looking for stonefly nymphs, mayfly nymphs, and caddisfly larvae. If they find all three types of immature insects, they rate the water quality as excellent. This water is suited for all human uses. If they find mayflies and caddisflies, but no stoneflies, then the water quality is considered good. If they find only caddisflies, then the water quality is rated as fair. If they don't find any of the three types of immature insects, the water quality is listed as poor.

Make a Connection

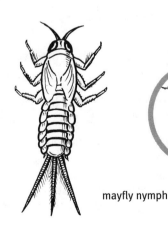

To see examples of aquatic creatures and learn how tolerant they are of pollution, go to www.iowater.net/ Benthickey.htm.

Insectigations! Game Board

As you hunt and capture insects and record your finds, you will notice patterns about where different insects live. Use this knowledge to create the game board for your own *Insectigations!* game.

Materials

1 piece of posterboard
Pencil
Markers

The posterboard will be your game board, showing the different habitats. Look through your journal to create a list of habitats where you have searched for insects. Your list might include backyard, grassy field, forest, pond, ocean, kitchen cupboard, and underground. Use your pencil to divide the board into sections for each type of habitat, making large areas for places you found a lot of insects, and smaller areas for habitats that didn't have as many insects. Sketch a trail that winds through all the habitats. This trail will be where you place your action cards, so it must be 3 inches (7.6 cm) wide so the cards will fit.

After you have an arrangement you like, use the markers to draw features of each area, such as grass and a house for the backyard, trees and rotting logs in the forest, water and cattails for the pond. Put the game board in a safe place until you have made all the action cards from the end of each chapter and are ready to play *Insectigations!*

Action Cards

Materials

2 3-by-5-inch (7.6-by-12.7-cm)
  index cards
Scissors
Pen
Envelope

Cut the index cards in half so that you have 4 2½-by-3-inch (6.3-by-7.6-cm) cards. Write the following actions based on finding or catching insects, one to a card. Place all four cards (including the blank one) into the envelope for safekeeping until you are ready to create your *Insectigations!* game.

- Oh no! You were harvested in the garden and made into surprise stew. Go back to start.
- Someone set out a pit trap. Roll the thorax die. If you are an insect that normally crawls, lose one turn.

- You got caught in a sweep net by an inexperienced entomologist. If a roll of the abdomen die shows you have a stinger or an ovipositor, take an extra turn.

After you have practiced all the finders tips and tricks, you will amaze your family and friends with the number and variety of insects you find, no matter where you are. Of course, the next question is, what are you going to do with all the insects you find? Read on to discover some interesting possibilities.

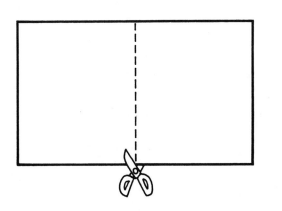

Here comes a fly swatter! If a roll of the head die doesn't show big compound eyes, lose one turn.

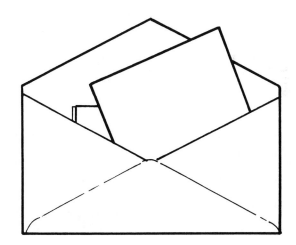

7

Keepers

Since insects have been around for so long, it's not surprising that ancient artifacts show human-insect interactions. A painting made by cave dwellers in Spain more than 15,000 years ago depicts someone raiding a honeybee hive. There are 4,000-year-old hieroglyphics in pyramids showing Egyptians honoring dung beetles as their sun god. Cicadas carved of jade that are more than 2,500 years old have been found as part of Chinese burials, and Chinese folklore suggests that people believed cicadas could help them be reborn.

Within recorded history, humans have used bees for honey and beeswax, silkworms for silk, and a protective covering of resin made by scale insects in India and Burma to make shellac.

Insects have also provided the inspiration for inventions, including paper, sonar, and chemical weapons. The question is, once *you* start catching insects, what do you want to do with them? Options include: keeping them as pets, using them in experiments and research projects, creating an insect collection, harvesting their products, selling them as a business or, of course, simply observing them and then letting them go!

Bug Business

Japan is a small island that is home to millions of people.

There isn't much room for pet dogs and cats, so many Japanese people keep crickets, beetles, and fireflies as pets instead. The insects are sold in pet shops, train stations, department stores, and one company even puts them in vending machines. While most pet owners are happy to pay as little as $4.50 for an average-sized beetle, other pet owners think that bigger is better and are willing to pay extra to get a large beetle. Even so, it is hard to believe that in August 1999, a Japanese businessman paid an insect dealer $90,000 for one super-sized stag beetle.

Temporary Terrarium

There's no doubt about it—if you watch insects long enough, you can witness some fantastic things, such as watching a praying mantis catch and eat another insect, a caterpillar spinning a cocoon, or two male stag beetles battling over a female. If you are very lucky and observant, you might see these things in the wild. But it is much easier if the insects are in an enclosed space.

It is important to remember that insects are living creatures and a vital part of our ecosystems. If you have caught some insects that you would like to observe for a few days, the best way to see how they really act is to duplicate, as close as you can, what their home is like. They need food, water, shelter, and space. For mealworms and crickets, these four things are pretty easy to supply. But dragonflies

require too much space, and scientists are still trying to determine what a male lightning beetle eats. Then there are the hornets and wasps, which are never good candidates for terrariums.

Materials

Soil

Large, clear container with lid (aquarium, hamster cage, or large plastic food container)

Pebbles

Sand

Small, green plant

Dry leaves

Branches

Wet sponge

Jar lid

Dry cereal

Pieces of fruit (apple, banana, and more)

Place the loose soil on the bottom of one half, and the peb-

bles and sand on the bottom of the other half of your container. Plant a small, green plant in the soil. Add some loose, dry leaves for shelter. Stick in a few branches for climbing and a wet sponge on a jar lid for water. Dry cereal, apple slices, and banana pieces will provide food for many insects, while others will eat each other. Top it all off with a tight-fitting lid with plenty of breathing holes. You might also want to cover at least part of the terrarium with dark paper or cloth to make your night-active insects more active during your day.

Plant eaters need fresh food, and some are very picky. If you catch an insect on a plant, make sure you put

some of the same plant in the terrarium. If you are not sure what plant your insects will eat, gather several different kinds from the area where they were captured. Watch what they eat and replace those plants every day with fresh ones.

If you have a predatory insect such as a praying mantis, you will either need to catch or raise food for it. You can buy mealworms

Make a Connection

Visit www.centralpets.com or check out *Pet Bugs: A Kid's Guide to Catching and Keeping Touchable Insects* by Sally Kneidel (New York: John Wiley and Sons, 1994) for more information about keeping insects as pets.

and crickets at many pet stores, or use your sweep net to catch its daily dinner.

If you are trying to keep aquatic insects alive, make sure you have a large jar or aquarium full of pond water and plants. Put some mud and rocks on the bottom for insects to take cover. If you need more liquid, don't put in water straight from a faucet. Let tap water sit in a jar for at least 24 hours before carefully adding it to your aquarium. Otherwise, the chlorine that is added to make drinking water safe for humans will likely kill all your insects. Some aquatic insects will eat fish food, while others need to eat insects and small creatures to survive.

Dead Insect Collections

Many people, universities, and museums have insect collections. Some people collect insects as souvenirs from places they have

Journal Notes

I started my terrarium on this date:

_____

I started my terrarium with these insects:

_____

Here's what each insect likes to eat:

_____

Here's what I've seen each of them do:

_____

Make a Connection

Look in the front of *A Field Guide to Insects: American North of Mexico (Peterson Field Guide Series)* by Richard E. White and Donald J. Borror (Houghton Mifflin, 1998) for specific instructions on how to label and preserve insects as part of a true collection.

traveled, while others collect them as a challenge, such as who can collect the most kinds of crickets. Museums and universi-

ties have insect collections for people to enjoy and for scientific research. Collections also help to show change over long periods of time. Researchers can measure insect species that were captured more than 100 years ago and see if they are bigger or smaller than ones found in the same area today. Whether you want to collect insects for a hobby, as a sport, or to do research, one thing is certain: it's easier to examine, identify, and draw an insect that doesn't move!

There are so many of most kinds of insects that you will not be threatening the survival of an insect species by capturing and keeping one as part of a collection. However, you should never take more insects than you need. Also, never take an insect if it's the only one you see in one place at one time.

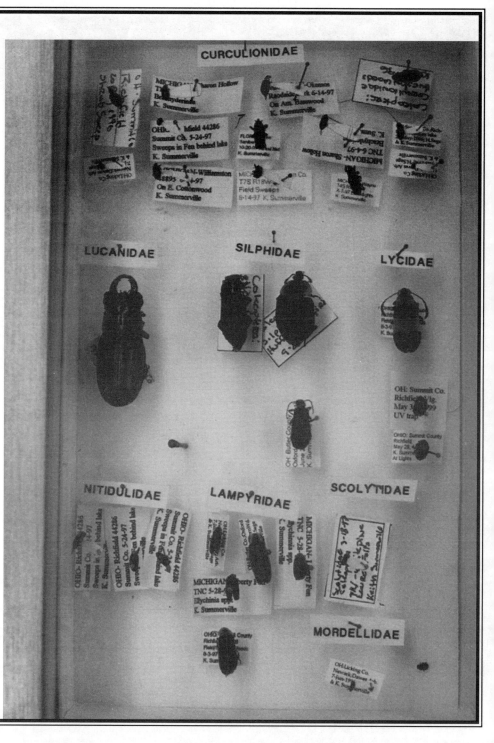

Properly mounted insects include information about when and where they are found.

You Saw What?

When ancient explorers traveled to new lands, they returned with stories about everything they had seen—including new insects. As the stories were passed from person to person, sometimes the descriptions were changed a bit, either by accident or to make the story a little better. Artists would try to draw the animals described, without ever having seen them. Sometimes, this created very unusual looking animals.

Materials

Insect
Paper
Pencil
A friend

Do you think the artist who drew this was looking at a fly or listening to someone else's description of what a fly looks like?

Look carefully at a real insect, then write a detailed description of it, without naming what type it is. Describe what it looks like and how it acts. Include all the details you can, such as it was carrying something four times its size, or has eyes that take up most of its head. Give your description to a friend (without telling him or her it is an insect) and ask your friend to try to draw what you described.

In later years, explorers including James Cook, who traveled to Antarctica, and Charles Darwin didn't bring back just stories. They collected actual insects to help people understand the new lands they explored.

For more than 50 years, moviemakers have entertained audiences with insects. Scary movies have featured oversized moths *(Mothra)*, praying mantises *(The Deadly Mantis)*, and cockroaches *(The Mimic 2)*. Animators have also had fun creating ants, grasshoppers, caterpillars, and fleas that sing, dance, and invent things in films including *A Bug's Life* and *Antz*. If you were making a movie, what would you have this large chestnut weevil do?

Jerry A. Payne, USDA ARS

Bug Business

For many years, people have hunted, killed, and mounted insects to sell to collectors and educators. John Assimwe in Uganda, Africa, walked through his country's dense forests collecting insects. He pickled stag beetles in alcohol and pinned rare butterflies to stiff boards, then mailed them to collectors and researchers around the world. He sold some butterflies for $20 each, and a rare beetle in good condition for almost $100. But tracking through the jungle is hard work, and finding a specific insect isn't always easy.

Now there is a new twist on the business. To help preserve rain-forests and other important habitats, some governments and companies are teaching people how to raise insects that are found in their areas. John Assimwe is now working with a United States businessman to start an insect farm. The farm will have workers who tend the native plants that provide food for the insects, and feed and breed the insects. When the insects die, the workers will mount and sell them. When organized correctly, these insect farms will help sustain the native habitat and wildlife while providing people with jobs.

Endangered Insects

In 2004, there were 35 insects listed on the federal endangered species list. This means there is a limited number of each insect, or very few places where the insects can now be found. How do scientists determine an insect is endangered? This is where collections come in handy.

Before natural land is developed, scientists survey the site to determine what lives there. If they find an insect (or any other animal or plant) they haven't seen anywhere else, they do some research. They ask museums and universities to look in their collections to see if they have an example of the insect in question. The little tags that label each specimen help the researchers understand where the insect has been captured before. Then they can visit those places to see if the insect can still be found there or not. If they can't find the insect anywhere else, or find only limited numbers of it, they can ask that the insect be classified as an endangered species.

How does this affect humans? If you owned land that was home to an endangered species, you might not be able to build a home on it, farm it, or change it in any way that could harm the insect. This makes some landowners mad. They want to know why it is so important to save one more kind of fly, or beetle, or flea.

The reason scientists believe it is important to save every species they can is the same reason you keep all the parts that come with a new bike you assemble. You might not know what each part is for, but you don't want to be missing a part you need. There are so many insects that haven't been studied, entomologists don't know what might happen if one species of insect disappeared.

For example, what would happen if all the endangered California Delhi sand flies disappeared? Perhaps they are the only insect that pollinates a certain type of plant. So if the fly disappears, that plant will, too. And maybe that plant produces a chemical that someday will be discovered to be a cure for a disease. If the fly disappears and therefore so does that plant, then we'll never discover this cure.

Make a Connection

To check out the list of endangered animals (including insects), visit http://endangered.fws.gov.

What can you do if you want or need an insect collection, but don't want to catch or kill any insects? There are plenty of other ways to create a large and unique insect collection.

If you want to have a collection of real insects:

• Look in the light fixtures and windowsills in your home and school. Most of them have insects just dying to be a part of your collection. Use clear tape to lift them out and put them on index cards for study.

• Look on the front of a car. From the spring to the fall, insects from butterflies to beetles can be found smashed on the windshield and grill. Pry them off using toothpicks, then use clear tape to attach them to index cards. If you want to try to identify them, check out the book *That Gunk on Your Car: A Unique Guide to Insects of North America* by Mark Hostetler (Berkeley, CA: Ten Speed Press, 1997).

• Collect shed exoskeletons (cicadas are particularly easy to find).

If you want to have a collection *about* insects:

• Collect insect stickers
• Collect insect toys
• Collect insect jewelry
• Collect insect stamps

In October 1999, the U.S. Postal Service came out with the Insects and Spiders 3-D stamps. Although you can't buy them at the post office anymore, you might be able to find one of these (or an insect stamp from a different country) on an old letter or card your parents have. Cut around the stamp, then soak it in water until the stamp slides off the paper. Look on the back of the U.S. stamps for information about the arthropod on the front.

INSECTS & SPIDERS

Fly-Tying a Big Bug

Some people who fish don't use worms or minnows as bait. They use lures, which are fake animals. Most lures are called flies, even though they might be made to imitate minnows, frogs, beetles, grasshoppers, ants, aquatic insects, and their larvae. Some fishing flies are smaller than your pinkie nail, while others are bigger than your whole thumb. Some flies are made to sink to the bottom of the water, and others float or are skipped along the surface. Fly-tying is a hobby, an art, and a business. Anglers (people who fish) tie a similar but smaller version of the pattern below to use when they are fishing for bluegill.

Materials

Scissors
Sponge
Wire hanger hook (left over from making sweep net on page 71)

This fly was made to look like a caddisfly. It would be used to attract trout and other insect-eating fish.   Fly tied by Craig Evans

Glue
1 18-inch (46-cm) piece of yarn
1 2-inch (5-cm) piece of yarn
2 twist ties (from loaves of bread)
2 plastic eyes

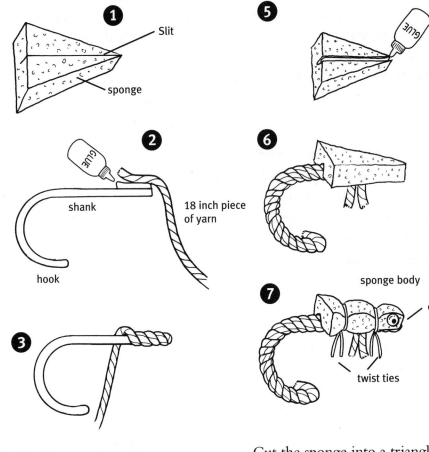

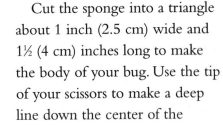

Cut the sponge into a triangle about 1 inch (2.5 cm) wide and 1½ (4 cm) inches long to make the body of your bug. Use the tip of your scissors to make a deep line down the center of the

wet fly

nymph

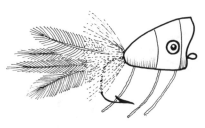

basspepper

biggest side of the sponge, without cutting all the way through. Set the sponge aside. Starting at the tip of the straight part of the wire (shank), apply a 1-inch (2.5-cm) line of glue. Place one inch (2.5 cm) of the long piece of yarn on the glue, with the remaining part hanging off the tip. After the glue dries, hold the hook part of the wire in one hand, and wrap the hanging piece of yarn around the wire, starting at the glued tip and ending on the hook tip. Wrap any leftover yarn back over already wrapped wire, and glue it in place.

Bend the small piece of yarn in half, and glue it over the middle of the shank. This will make the middle legs of your big bug. Squeeze a line of glue in the slit you made in the sponge. Position the sponge so that the yarn legs will be under the middle of it and the narrow tip points toward the shank tip of the wire. Press the sponge down on the wire. Wrap one twist tie about one-third of the way past the tip of the sponge to make the head and the first pair of legs. Wrap the second twist tie about two-thirds of the back to separate the thorax and abdomen and create the third pair of legs. Glue eyes on the front and your big bug fishing fly is done.

After you have made a basic bug, you can create fancier flies by decorating your sponge or adding small feathers and bits of fur under the twist ties.

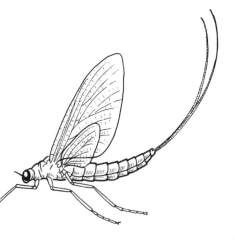

Mayfly

Mayfly Mania

In the summertime, you might head to a river or lake only to find it, and you, covered with flying insects. Before you start swatting, look closely to see how many tails the pests have. If they have two or three long tails, you are in the midst of mayfly mania.

Mayflies spend most of their lives as nymphs underwater. The nymphs have two or three tails, too. Sometimes millions of mayfly nymphs undergo their last molt and emerge as adults on the same day. There are true stories of so many mayflies covering roads that drivers have to turn their headlights on during the day.

But the mania is short-lived. Mayfly adults do not have working mouthparts, so they only live for one to three days. This is just long enough to find a mate, lay eggs, and provide a feast for the birds, bats, fishes, and frogs in the area.

Action Cards

Materials

2 3-by-5-inch (7.6-by-12.7-cm)
   index cards
Scissors
Pen
Envelope

Cut the index cards in half so that you have 4 2½-by-3-inch (6.3-by-7.6-cm) cards. Write the following actions based on insect collections, one to a card. Place all four cards (including the blank one) into the envelope for safe-keeping until you are ready to create your *Insectigations!* game.

- Tourist has started a moth collection. If a roll of any insect die shows you're a moth, go back to start.

- Angler is looking for bait. If a roll of any insect die shows you could live under a rock, go back 4 spaces.

- Entomologist doing a land survey discovers you are an endangered species. Your land is protected, so move ahead 10 spaces.

While finding, catching, and keeping insects is a lot of fun, sometimes it feels good just to sit back and let the insects come to you. Learn how to make your yard an insect magnet with plants, puddles, and shelters in the next chapter on insect gardening.

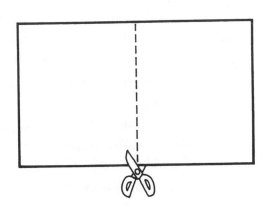

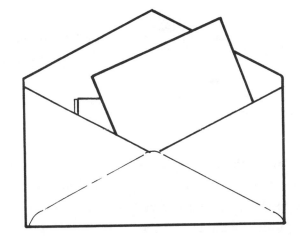

Here comes a fly swatter! If a roll of the head die doesn't show big compound eyes, lose one turn.

Insect Gardening

Instead of spending all your time searching for insects, you can plant a garden to attract insects and watch them come to you! An insect garden can be as small as a pot of flowers in a calm, sunny place or as large as your whole backyard. The thing to remember is that all insects need food, water, and shelter. The more variety you can provide of each of these, the more types of insects you can attract.

Food

Some insects eat plants, some insects eat dead or rotting things, and some insects eat animals (usually other insects). It is easiest to provide food for the plant-eating insects, but don't just think of flowers. Insects eat all the parts of plants. Beetle grubs often munch the roots; caterpillars, aphids, and spittlebugs dine on leaves and stems; and butterflies, moths, and honeybees head for the nectar-filled flowers. Flower feeders are usually garden visitors, flying in to get a meal, then flying away as soon as they have finished. Meanwhile, those insects that dine on the other plant parts might stay on one plant in your garden for their whole lives!

Since most insects have fuzzy eyesight, it is easier for them to find big groups of similar plants. If your insect garden is small, you might attract more insects if you have just one type and color of plant. If you have a large garden area and want many different insects, include a wide variety of plants, grouped by color.

Try some native plants (plants that grow naturally in your area) and ones with different flower shapes, colors, smells, and blooming times. Day-active (diurnal) insects use shape and color to decide which flowers to visit. Bees like yellow, blue, and lavender flowers that have a tube-shape, such as jewelweed, foxglove, lupine, and snapdragons. Butterflies prefer red, orange, yellow, and purple flowers with large flat heads that give them a place to land. Good flowers include milkweed, butterfly weed, yarrow, columbine, and purple aster. Night-active (nocturnal) insects like moths look for large, light-colored flowers or flowers with strong smells. Good plants include evening primrose, moonflower, bouncing Bet, Dame's rocket, and petunia.

As soon as the plant-eating insects are in your garden, look for the predatory insects. Ladybugs, lacewings, and praying mantises might stop by to see if they can catch some dinner.

Pollination Process

If there were no insects, there would be less cocoa, peaches, strawberries, apples, nuts, oranges, cherries, other plant fruits, or cotton. Plants produce edible or useful fruit to encourage animals (including humans) to help move their seeds to new places. You move seeds every time you wash purple bird poop off the family car or have a watermelon seed spitting contest. Although insects don't *make* any of the seeds or fruits, they are an important part of the process.

How do insects help? They pollinate plants—the first step in seed production. Think of a flower as a seed factory. To make a seed, a flower must put together two important parts, the ova and the pollen. The ova are surrounded by nectar deep inside the flower in a place called the ovary. The pollen is sitting on a stamen outside the ovary, by a door called the stigma. Since most flowers cannot move,

Gross Entomology:
Pass the Poop, Please

Gardeners often use animal droppings as fertilizer for their plants. Nutrients that pass through an animal are taken up by the plants, helping them grow stronger and healthier. What gardeners might not realize is that many insects like to eat poop, too! Dung beetles roll mammal poop into balls then lay their eggs inside. Satyr butterflies feed on bird droppings. So if you want to create a garden good for both plants and insects, make sure you add the poop!

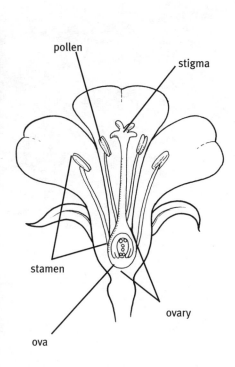

pollen

stigma

stamen

ova

ovary

Have you ever noticed signs painted on streets? Arrows, colors, shapes, and words give drivers directions. Some flowers have signs, too. They use circles of color, flashy landing spots, lines, and ultraviolet paths to guide bees and other insects to the nectar. The dark spot on this pansy is a sign to lead insects to its nectar.

they need a delivery vehicle. This is the job for the insects.

As an insect visits a flower to get some nectar, it brushes by the stamens. Some pollen rubs off on its body. (You can see this for yourself if you wrap a piece of dark felt around a stick and brush it over a flower. Look at the pollen collected on the felt.) At the next flower, the insect delivers some pollen right to the stigma (the ovary door) as it gets a drink of nectar. The plant takes over from there, and a seed is started.

Water

Like all living creatures, insects need water to survive. Mosquitoes, mayflies, dragonflies, and darners lay their eggs in water. Water striders, whirligigs, and diving beetles use water as their hunting grounds for dinner. Bees, flies, and leafhoppers simply need water to drink. For those insects that don't live in or near water, a single drop can be more than enough to satisfy their thirst. The trouble is, where do you find a single drop of water on a hot, dry day?

If your yard already has a birdbath in it, there are a few things you can do to make it insect friendly. Add some sticks or leaves to the water so insects that accidentally fall in can climb out without waiting for you to rescue them. To make the birdbath people-friendly, change the water

The rocks act as warming spots while the sponges hold the mineral water.

every other day. Otherwise, mosquitoes might decide it is a good place to lay their eggs!

A better way to provide water for insects is to soak a washcloth or hand towel in clean water

every morning. Hang it over a branch or on a clothesline and watch flies, leafhoppers, bees, and other insects come for a drink.

Most butterflies and some other insects get the water they

need from the food they eat. But they do look for seeps (moist soil or sand) where they can slurp up mineral water, that is, water that has important nutrients that have been released from the soil.

Butterfly Puddles

By creating a watering hole just for butterflies, you can do these insects a favor and get the chance to take a better look at them.

Materials

Rich topsoil

Shallow dish, such as a plant
    pot holder, pie pan, or tray

Several flat rocks of different
    colors

Markers or paints

Sponges

Scissors

Water

Spread a thin layer of soil in the bottom of the dish. Decorate the rocks with the markers or paint, then arrange them in the dish. Cut the sponges into designs and place them between the rocks. Wet the sponges so that some water seeps into the soil below, but not so much that there is standing water. Place

your butterfly puddle in a sunny area near flat-headed flowers such as zinnias or Queen Anne's lace. Try to keep it out of the wind, and make sure it stays moist by checking it daily.

Journal Notes

When do butterflies land on the dark-colored rocks? (When it is sunny? Cloudy? Cool? Morning? Evening?)

When do they land on light-colored rocks?

Insects are cold-blooded. They use their surroundings to regulate their body temperatures. Watch your garden just as the sun reaches it on a cool morning. You might see insects warming themselves in the sun. Morning is a great time to catch and observe insects. If the air cooled considerably during the night, the insects are likely to be moving much slower.

Shelter

Insects use a wide variety of strategies in seeking shelter. Ants tunnel underground, beetles hide under rocks, bees construct hives in hollow spaces, paper wasps build nests in protected corners. Underwater, caddisfly larvae create a kind of glue to stick small sticks and pebbles together, making their own portable home. Although you can't build a home for each and every insect, here are things to consider when you are planning your garden.

- Plants with wide leaves provide more protection than plants with narrow leaves.
- Piles of leaves, rocks, and bark give crawling insects places to hide.
- Rotting logs or branches are home to many types of insects.

- Each fall, many insects lay their eggs on or near their host plants—the ones their babies will want to eat. If you want to see more insects each spring, leave a thick layer of leaves and your plant stalks standing after they have died. That way, new insects won't have to look for your garden the next year; they will already be there.

One caution: if you use potted plants in your insect garden, leave them outdoors when the weather gets colder. Otherwise, you might get some unexpected insects as houseguests!

The small tag on a monarch's wing doesn't hurt its ability to fly, and it helps researchers track its migration path. Darrin Siefkin

106

Monarch Migration Mystery

Dr. Urquhart at the University of Toronto had a problem. For 38 years he had been trying to find out what happened to monarch butterflies in the winter. Some scientists thought that only monarchs in the South survived cold winters, but monarchs could survive in the North during mild winters. Dr. Urquhart believed that since monarchs are tropical butterflies, they had to fly south each winter to escape the cold. Then each spring, they would fly north to find milkweed for their babies to eat. But he didn't have any proof.

In 1937, Dr. Urquhart started sticking small labels with his address on the wings of monarchs. When people mailed tagged butterflies to him, he marked where they were found on a map. It looked like most monarchs were going to Texas, or maybe Mexico. He found 3,000 volunteers to help him, but still couldn't find many live butterflies. Where were they? Finally, in 1972, his wife Norah wrote some articles for Mexican newspapers, asking people there to help. Ken Brugger read one of the articles. He worked at an underwear factory in Mexico City and had seen some monarchs around the countryside. He offered to tag monarchs and look for their winter home. Two years passed. In January 1975, Ken and his wife, Catalina, followed local farmers and loggers hiking up the ancient volcanoes of the Sierra Madre. When they reached a clearing, they saw an estimated 15 million monarchs resting on oyamel fir trees. It was the first record of outsiders finding the monarchs' winter hideaway.

The next year, Dr. Urquhart went to Mexico. "What a glorious, incredible sight!" he said. Then he watched a tree branch covered with monarchs fall to the ground. As he bent over to examine them, he noticed one with a label. It had been tagged in Minnesota—proof that the butterfly had migrated from nearly 2,000 miles to the north.

The discovery of the monarch's winter home was important, but Dr. Urquhart's work wasn't done. He picked up a butterfly, rubbed a few scales off a wing, and attached a bright pink tag. Now it was time to see how far north these monarchs went in the spring.

Although Dr. Urquhart died in 2002, researchers today are still tagging monarchs and studying their migration.

Make a Connection

To learn more about monarchs and how you can help by tagging monarchs, go to www.MonarchWatch.org.

Antifreeze

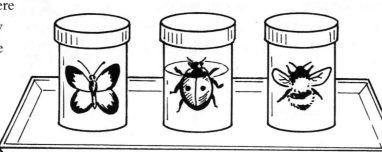

In the parts of the world where the temperature drops below freezing, adult insects do one of three things as winter approaches: they migrate (monarchs), lay eggs and die (grasshoppers), or adapt and spend the entire winter as an adult (mourning cloak butterfly and box elder bug). To survive the cold weather, insects that overwinter as adults lose body moisture, and some of them produce glycerol, a type of alcohol that acts as an antifreeze.

Materials

3 clear film canisters with lids
Stickers
Water
Rubbing alcohol

Plate or tray

Decorate the film canisters with the stickers so you can tell them apart. Put all three canisters in a sink or bowl. Fill one canister completely full with water, then snap on the lid. Fill one canister half full with water, then snap on the lid. Fill the third canister completely full with rubbing alcohol and snap on the lid. Put all three canisters on a plate or tray and put the tray in a freezer overnight. In the morning, check on your "insects."

Never drink rubbing alcohol or car antifreeze. Rubbing alcohol can make you very sick, and antifreeze can kill you.

Journal Notes

What happened to the canister completely filled with water?

What happened to the canister half-filled with water?

What happened to the canister filled with rubbing alcohol?

When water freezes, it expands. When people suffer from severe frostbite, the water in their skin and muscle cells freezes, then bursts the cells, causing tissue and muscle damage. Insects lose moisture, giving the remaining water room to expand. Alcohols are a type of antifreeze. Antifreeze is a solution that keeps liquids from freezing and expanding. Insect antifreeze keeps their blood from freezing and breaking their bodies.

Bug Bumps

While you are looking for insects in your garden, you might notice strange-looking bumps on a few plants. Some wasps, flies, and aphids lay eggs in a certain part of a plant. The plant grows around them, forming a snug home called a gall. If you open a gall carefully, you might see insect larvae wiggling around. Look for galls on tree leaves and plant stems around your home. Hackberry, oak, hickory, and maple trees often have galls, as do goldenrod stems and grape leaves. Since it can be very hard to identify the larvae, tie a piece of sheer curtain around the unopened gall. Check back on the gall every few days until the adult has emerged. Sketch the gall and the animal in your journal. Each gall producer makes its own special kind of gall. Once you know who made what, you will have an easy way to identify both plants and animals.

The nipple galls on these hackberry leaves are home to psyllid fly larvae.

Plan Your Garden

Now that you know a bit about what insects need, you can plan your garden. First decide on the best place for your garden, and what types of insects you want to attract. It is easiest to find information about how to attract butterflies and moths, but that doesn't mean you can't plant a garden for grasshoppers or stinkbugs if you want to. A general gardening guide such as *Landscaping for Wildlife & Air Quality* by Carrol L. Henderson, et al.

(Minnesota Bookstore, 1987) provides great background information for almost all types of insects. Look in your library, bookstore, or online for more specific details about your favorite type of insect. For example, imagine you want to watch ambush bugs grab and eat unsuspecting insects. You read a book about ambush bugs and learn they are often found in goldenrod plants, which are a favorite food for flower flies (syrphids), butterflies, and skippers (a

special group of butterflies). Your next step would be to find a type of goldenrod plant that grows where you live.

Continue keeping notes in your journal after your garden is planted. Do the butterflies seem to like one plant better than another? Do all the plants survive? When did you see your first predatory insect? Did any other animals (such as spiders, centipedes, and millipedes) move into your garden as well?

Journal Notes

This is the best location for my insect garden:
This is the best place for these reasons:_____
I want these insects to visit or live in my garden: _____
These are the insects I've found in my garden: _____

_____

These insects like to eat

_____

These insects have other special needs, including these: _____

_____

_____

_____

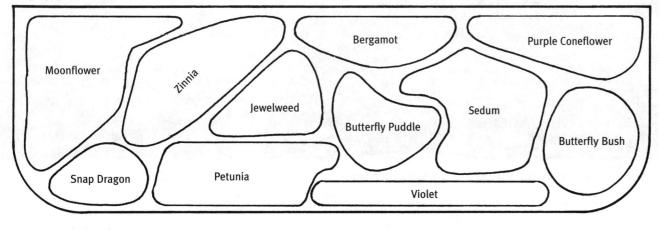

Plant tall flowers in the back, medium ones in the middle and short ones in front.
Don't forget to include a place for your butterfly puddle.

Insect Calendar

People haven't always used paper calendars to indicate the day, month, and season. Before paper was even invented, people used the position of the sun, phases of the moon, and the appearance and disappearance of plants and animals to guide them through the seasons. For example, people knew that once they heard the katydids start singing, the first frost was only about six weeks away. This study of recurring events in nature is called phenology (fi-NOL-a-ji). A garden is one of the best places to practice phenology.

Materials
Calendar
Pencil
Insect garden

Some people call phenology the science of appearances and disappearances. To be a phenologist, you need to notice when each type of insect and plant in your garden appears, sings, migrates, and disappears. Since it is easier to notice when something starts, such as the first day you notice cicadas singing, sometimes it is best if you record every insect and plant you notice, every day. When you look back over your calendar to check for patterns, it will be easier to see the last day you heard a cricket sing or saw a butterfly.

Although it will take several years to collect enough information to look for patterns in your own garden, you can test the following observations made by other phenologists to see if they work in your area.

- Grasshopper eggs hatch when lilacs bloom.
- Mexican bean beetle larvae appear when foxglove flowers open.
- Wasps building nests in exposed places indicate a dry season.
- When you see a white butterfly, summer is almost here.

After collecting information for several years, you can make your own insect calendar, with stickers or drawings on the dates when you expect to see monarchs returning, when to listen for a cricket singing, and when the box elder bugs will start looking for a hibernation spot in your windowsills.

Insect Repellants

Although we rely on some insects to pollinate our food crops, other insects cause millions of dollars in damage to other crops. The Colorado potato beetle, boll weevil, cabbageworm, corn root worm, and tobacco horn worm (these "worms" are really caterpillars) are just five examples of insect pests. So while some entomologists have studied how to attract or encourage insect visitors, other entomologists have studied how to keep insects away. Putting up a sign or scarecrow doesn't work, and those blue-light bug zappers kill more harmless insects than mosquitoes, but there are plenty of other ways to limit the number of insects in a garden. Here are a few ideas:

- You can build houses for bats and insect-eating birds like wrens, bluebirds, and purple martins. (See Resources for more information.)
- You can put out traps and wrap tape, sticky-side out, around plant stems.
- You can buy and release ladybugs, lacewings, and praying mantises in your gardens.
- You can garden with plants that insects don't like.

Make a Connection

There is more information about companion plants and a list of good companion plant combinations at www.eapmcgill.ca/Publications/EAP55.htm.

Many insects won't visit fuzzy plants, such as lamb's ear. Chrysanthemums (kri-SAN-the-mum) produce the chemical pyrethrum, which is used as a pesticide to kill many insects, including the fleas on your cat or dog. Other plants also produce chemicals that insects don't like, so smart gardeners plant insect-repelling plants around the plants they want to keep. Here are some plants and the insects they naturally repel.

Plant	Repels These Insects
Nasturtium	Colorado Potato Beetle, Squash Bug, Whitefly
Garlic	Aphids, Flea Beetle, Japanese Beetle, Mexican Bean Beetle
Onion	Bean Leaf Beetle, Flea Beetle, Harlequin Bug, Squash Vine Borer
Mint	Ants, Aphids, Flea Beetle, Imported Cabbage Worm

Real Entomologists

Some people don't like to use chemicals to keep mosquitoes away, but they still don't want to get mosquito bites. So scientists are trying to find natural repellants. An entomologist at North Carolina State University has discovered that a chemical found in tomatoes seems to keep mosquitoes away. Researchers at Iowa State University are testing how well catnip oil works to do the same thing. To see if they are right, you can do some research of your own. The next time you are going outside for the evening, stop by your garden first. Rub a few leaves of crushed catnip on one arm and leg, and some crushed tomato on the other arm and leg. You may need to watch out for stray cats or tomato beetles, but those pesky mosquitoes might leave you alone!

Materials

2 3-by-5-inch (7.6-by-12.7-cm) index cards
Scissors
Pen
Envelope

Cut the index cards in half so that you have 4 2½-by-3-inch (6.3-by-7.6-cm) cards. Write the following actions related to insect gardens, one to a card. Place all four cards (including the blank one) into the envelope for safe-keeping until you are ready to create your *Insectigations!* game.

- Oh no! Got eaten by a praying mantis. Go back to start.
- If a roll of the head die shows you are a nectar eater, roll again.
- Overwintered on a plant stalk in the garden. Lose one turn.

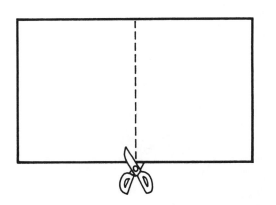

Here comes a fly swatter! If a roll of the head die doesn't show big compound eyes, lose one turn.

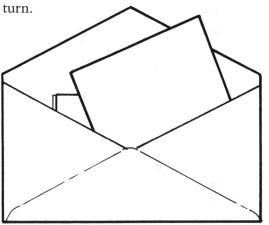

After a day of exploring, experimenting, and working in your insect garden, you decide to spend the evening sitting in a comfortable spot among your plants, flipping through your *Insectigations* journal. But you don't sit still long, for you remember you need to check your pit trap. After sketching and releasing the beetles and centipedes (even though they are insect imposters) that fell in the trap during the day, you look up just in time. A butterfly like the one you found as an egg, then raised to maturity, stops in its special puddle, then flits off to a flower before finding an evening resting spot. As the evening insect chorus starts to hum, you grab the bug buzzer tucked in your journal pocket and try to match the pulsing rhythm of the cicada song. It seems a shame that a day full of insect investigations has to end. Then you realize, maybe it doesn't. You head to the phone to invite some friends over for an incredible game of *Insectigations!* When they say they are on their way, you suddenly realize you need to put the game together. Better read on and get going!

Insectigations! The Game

2 to 4 players

If a single pair of flies were to breed, and all their babies survived and had more babies, and all those babies survived and had even more babies, then within a year—if you crammed all the flies' bodies together into a ball—the ball would be about 96 million miles in diameter! So, some insects have to die before they have a chance to mate and lay eggs. What causes them to die? The answer is on your action cards!

Materials

Game pieces	Dice
(see sidebar)	Tokens, such as plastic bugs,
Tape or glue	cicada exoskeletons, and
Marker	decorated bottle tops

Place the game board on the floor or a big table. Read through your action cards and decide in which habitat they would work best. For example, if you have a card about turning over rotten logs in a forest, that card should be in the forest habitat. After you have determined the best place for each action card, line them up in the trail area you made on the game board. It's OK to create more action cards or use the blank cards where you need them.

Once you have a path that goes through your habitats, tape the cards into place. Draw an oval as your starting square and label it "Egg." Draw an adult insect at the finish line of the path. Find a few friends and collect some exoskeletons or plastic bugs to use as your tokens and get ready to play!

The object of the game is to be the first one to make it from the start (Egg) to the finish (Adult). Here are the rules of the game:

1. Have each player roll a regular, numbered die. The one rolling the highest number goes first.
2. Each player takes a turn by rolling the numbered die and then moving his or her game token along the action card path.
3. Follow the instructions on the action card that you land on after moving the number you rolled on the die.
4. If a player lands on a space that is already occupied, it is time for a duel. Each player selects either the head or abdomen insect die to roll. (They can choose the same die.) If a player rolls a weapon (like a stinger or pincer), that player can send the other player back to start. If both players roll a weapon, they both go back to start. If neither one rolls a weapon, they both stay on the square.

Do you have the luck you need to survive as an insect? Roll the dice and see what happens.

Game Pieces

The instructions for creating all the parts you need are found in the following places.

Game board: See Chapter 6 on page 85.

Insect dice: See Chapter 2 on page 27.

Action cards: See the end of Chapters 2 through 8 on pages 31, 43, 55, 68, 87, 100, and 113).

Ten Common Insect Orders

With so many insects in the world, it would take a very thick book to identify every single one. Sometimes, the best you can do is figure out which order an insect belongs to. Insects are grouped by things they have in common. The order name usually gives you a clue to their common characteristics. This table will help you put the insects you find into the correct order.

Order Name (What It Means)	Familiar Members	Characteristics
Blattodea (flat body)	Roaches: cockroach, wood roach, Chinese roach	Flat oval bodies with long, hairlike antennae. Small heads are hidden by a visorlike shield, abdomen hidden by four wings that they rarely use. They are fast runners who prefer the dark.
Coleoptera (sheath wings)	Beetles: Water beetles, lightning beetles, June bugs, weevils	Bodies can be almost any shape or size, but they all have a hard "shell," with a straight line down the middle of the back. This shell is made by the first set of wings that act as covers for the clear flying set folded underneath. Chewing mouthparts, some with large mandibles. Antennae can be very short or very long, usually threadlike or clubbed.
Diptera (two wings)	Flies: housefly, mosquito, midge	Only order where all adults have only two, transparent wings. Small antennae, bristle-like or feathery, and very large eyes. Piercing, lapping, or sponging mouthparts. Soft body.
Ephemeroptera (living one day)	Mayfly	Four transparent wings, the first set much larger than the hind set, held up over the back when resting. The abdomen is long and slender with three hairlike "tails" at the end. Large eyes, no working mouthparts as adults.
Hemiptera (half wings)	True bugs: ambush bug, assassin bug, stink bug	Two pairs of wings. When resting, the first pair folds flat over the back, making a rough "X" pattern. The head on land-based bugs is usually small with small eyes and long antennae. Water-based bugs have large heads with large eyes and short antennae. All have piercing-sucking mouthparts that form a beak that is held under the body when not in use.
Homoptera (similar wing)	Cicadas, leafhoppers, froghoppers	Most have four wings that are all very similar. When they are not being used, the wings form a "tent" or "roof" over the stocky body. Very short antennae, medium eyes, and sucking beaklike mouths for feeding on plants.
Hymenoptera (Membranous wings)	Ants, bees, wasps	Only insects with stingers. Are often found in social groups. Two pairs of thin, transparent wings, with the hind wings usually smaller. Some adults have no wings. Many have hard bodies with a narrow connection between thorax and abdomen that forms a pinched waist. Chewing or chewing-sucking mouthparts, and usually medium to long antennae. Ants have small compound eyes while bees and wasps often have large ones.
Lepidoptera (scale wings)	Butterflies and moths	Four wings covered with tiny, often colorful scales. Abdomens are much longer than the thorax and usually stout. Smallish heads with large compound eyes, coiled-tube mouthparts, and long antennae. Butterflies usually have knobbed antennae, moths usually have feathery antennae.
Odonata (tooth + water)	Dragonflies and damselflies	Four nearly equal-sized transparent wings with many veins. Dragonflies hold their wings out to the side when resting, damselflies hold theirs up over the body. The thorax looks short and stocky when compared to the long, slender, tapering abdomen. Very large compound eyes, very short bristle-like antennae, and biting/chewing mouthparts.
Orthoptera (straight wing)	Grasshoppers, katydids, crickets, and mantids	Long legs in front (praying mantis), bent higher than the body at the knee on the hind pair (crickets, grasshoppers, katydids), or all over (walking stick). Females may have long ovipositor at end of abdomen. Chewing mouthparts, usually long antennae, very small to large compound eyes. Those with wings have a leathery first set with the second pair folded like a fan and often tucked to the sides of the body.

Glossary

abdomen: third (last) of the three main body parts of an insect.

amplitude: the measurement of the vertical size of a sound wave.

arthropod: an invertebrate with a segmented external skeleton and jointed legs; including insects, spiders, ticks, millipedes, centipedes, and crustaceans.

cerci: small hooklike structures at the end of the abdomen, often used in mating.

decomposer: an organism that helps break down dead plants and animals.

dilute: to make a liquid weaker by adding water.

ecosystem: a community of interacting plants and animals and the area they live in.

entomology: the study of insects.

exoskeleton: hardened outer skin of an insect and other arthropods.

frequency: how often something repeats itself.

function: how an item is used; the purpose for which something exists.

habitat: the kind of place that is natural for the life and growth of an animal or plant.

instar: the stage of development between two molts of an immature insect.

invertebrate: any animal lacking a backbone. Includes insects, spiders, worms, and many other animals.

larva: the stage of development between egg and pupa in an insect that undergoes complete metamorphosis. A larva is usually an active feeding stage of an insect and doesn't look like the adult in form.

mandible: a jaw.

metamorphosis: the development of an insect from egg to adult, during which it changes shape from one stage to the next.

nymph: the stages of growth between egg and adult of an insect that undergoes simple metamorphosis.

ocelli: simple eyes; larvae can detect some colors and shapes, while adult insects are sensitive to light and movement but cannot see images.

organ: a specific part of an animal that has a specialized function.

ovipositor: the egg-laying structure on the rear abdominal segment of a female insect.

periodical: occurring at regular time intervals.

pheromone: a chemical smell produced by insects to attract a mate or form a cooperative group.

predator: an animal that hunts, kills, and eats other animals.

pupa: the third stage of complete metamorphosis in insects during which a larva transforms into an adult.

spiracle: an external opening of the breathing system in an insect.

surface area: measurement of that part of an object that touches the air.

thorax: the body region of an insect between the head and abdomen, it has the legs and wings.

volume: the amount of space that something occupies.

vortex: a whirling mass of water, like a whirlpool.

Resources

Chapter 1: Getting Started
Insect Folklore

- www.bijlmakers.com/entomology/proverbs_insects.htm
  This site contains an extensive collection of both factual and fanciful insect proverbs from around the world.

- Kite, L. Patricia. *Insect Facts and Folklore*. Brookfield, CT: The Mill-brook Press, 2001.
  Aimed at student in grades 3 to 7, the pictures, stories, and information about twelve different insects provide a fascinating look at insect-human interactions through the ages and around the globe.

Drawing Insects

- Dubosque, Doug and Damon Reinagle. *Draw Insects*. Columbus, NC: Peel Productions, 1997.
  Targeted to grades 4 to 8, this book provides lessons for creating detailed pencil drawings of over 80 arthropods. It also includes classification and habitat information about each creature.

- Masiello, Ralph. *Bug Drawing Book*. Watertown, MA: Charlesbridge, 2005.
  Written for children ages 5 to 9, this book provides simple instructions for drawing nine different adult insects, a caterpillar, chrysalis, and a spider and its web.

- Glausiusz, Josie. *Buzz: The Intimate Bond Between Humans and Insects*. San Francisco, CA: Chronicle Books, 2004.
  Many instructors encourage beginning artists to look at other drawings or photos as they learn the basics. *Buzz* features stunning photos and scanning electron micrographs of insects, giving readers an eyeful of details that would otherwise be missed.

- www.life.uiuc.edu/entomology/egsa/ifff.html
  In conjunction with its annual Insect Fear Film Festival, the University of Illinois at Urbana-Champaign hosts a thematic insect art contest for students grades K to 12. You'll find the rules, information, and an entry form on this Web site.

- www.si.edu/resource/faq/nmnh/buginfo/start.htm
  As part of its educational outreach efforts, the Smithsonian National Museum of Natural History offers profiles of various career opportunities, including that of an insect artist.

Chapter 2: Body Basics
About Abdomens

- The Firefly Project, 103 Wiltshire Drive, Oak Ridge, TN 37830, 888-520-1272, e-mail: fireflyproject@yahoo.com
  The direct address for the company that pays people to collect fireflies for research.

Mighty Muscles

- http://ufbir.ifas.ufl.edu/
  You can either view or contribute to the University of Florida at Gainesville Department of Entomology's list of 39 insect records, from the fastest flier to the smallest eggs.

- www.ftexploring.com/think/superbugs_p2.html
  A more thorough explanation (with illustrations) of how insect muscle use compares to human muscle use.

What's Bugging You

- www.csrees.usda.gov/Extension/index.html
  As part of the Cooperative State Research, Education, and Extension Service, many county extension offices assist residents with insect identification of local species. You can also find the number to your local extension office under "Extension Services" in the county government section of your phone book.

- *Insects and Spiders: National Audubon Society's Pocket Guide.* NY: Chanticleer Press, Inc., 1988.

- Kavanagh, James. *Bugs and Slugs: An Introduction to Familiar Invertebrates. Pocket Naturalist.* Chandler, AZ: Waterford Press, Inc., 2002.

- Leahy, Christopher. *Insects: A Concise Field Guide to 200 Common Insects of North America. Peterson's First Guides.* NY: Houghton Mifflin, 1987.

- McGavin, George C. *Insects: Spiders and Other Terrestrial Arthropods. Dorling Kindersley Handbooks.* NY: Dorling Kindersley Inc., 2000.

- Zim, Herbert S. Ph.D., and Clarence Cottam, Ph.D. *Insects: A Guide to Familiar American Insects. A Golden Guide.* NY: Golden Press, 1987.

Chapter 3: Metamorphic Magic
Complete Metamorphosis

- Wright, Amy Bartlett. *Peterson's First Guides: Caterpillars.* NY: Houghton Mifflin, 1993.
  Identification of caterpillars, including their habitat and food preferences and their final adult form.

- www.bijlmakers.com/entomology/metamorphosis.htm
  A computer-animated version of the complete metamorphosis of a butterfly.

Chapter 4: Sense-sational
Vision

- www.toledo-bend.com/colorblind/Ishihara.html
  The direct site for a standard test for color perception with links to helpful sites that have further information.

- www.colorvisiontesting.com
  Information about what it means to be colorblind, how to test young children for color perception, and suggestions for inclusive educational strategies.

- http://cvs.anu.edu.au/andy/beye/beyehome.html
  View computer-modeled bee vision with a selection of preloaded images or enter your own design.

Chapter 5: Can We Talk?

- www.naturesongs.com

  A virtual library of animal sounds, many accompanied by a picture and explanation of how and when the sound was recorded.

- www.wfu.edu/academics/biology/batsandbugs

  Information, activities, pictures, current research projects, and links about insect hearing at the Wake Forest University Bats and Bugs site.

Chapter 6: Finders
Gross Entomology: Pantry Pests

- www.cfsan.fda.gov/~dms/dalbook.html

  Download the U.S. Food and Drug Administration Center for Food Safety and Applied Nutrition Food Defect Action Level booklet to find out more about the allowable levels of insect pieces and parts found in your food.

- www.ent.iastate.edu/misc/insectsasfood.html

  If you are interested in adding cheap protein to your diet, this site offers recipes and links to companies that market edible insects.

Water We Looking For?

- http://biorobots.cwru.edu

  This Case Western Research University site explains its research into insect motion and displays its models of cockroach robots.

- www.iowater.net/Benthickey.htm

  In addition to providing graphics that aid in the identification of aquatic insects and other invertebrates, this site features information about starting your own water quality monitoring project.

Chapter 7: Keepers

- http://endangered.fws.gov/

  A continually updated list of animals on the federal endangered species list with links to information about the plans to monitor or improve the endangered populations.

- www.centralpets.com

  A large site with the goal of providing links to articles about the appropriate care information for all the nearly 15,000 animal species (including insects) currently kept as captive pets.

- Kneidel, Sally. *Pet Bugs: A Kid's Guide to Catching and Keeping Touchable Insects.* NY: John Wiley and Sons, 1994.

  Information about and instructions for capturing and keeping 26 kinds of common arthropods, including several types of insects.

- Zakowski, Connie. *The Insect Book: A Basic Guide to the Collection and Care of Common Insects for Young Children.* Highland City, FL: Rainbow Books, 1996.

  An elementary guide to capturing, identifying, and housing 28 common insects.

Dead Insect Collections

- http://entwebclemson.edu/museum

  Take an insect museum virtual tour, selecting which insects you want to examine more closely with the click of a mouse.

- www.mnh.si.edu/museum/VirtualTour/Tour/Second/InsectZoo/index.html

  The Smithsonian Institution's National Museum of Natural History in Washington, D.C. has an incredible exhibit area in the O. Orkin Insect Zoo. If you are not able to visit the museum in person, you can use the Web address to take a virtual tour online.

- Hostetler, Mark, PhD. *That Gunk on Your Car: A Unique Guide to Insects of North America.* Berkeley, CA: Ten Speed Press, 1997.

  A funny book that includes habitat and life cycle information about insects that are often found splattered on the front end of a vehicle.

- White, Richard E., and Donald J. Borror. *A Field Guide to Insects: American North of Mexico.* NY: Houghton Mifflin, 1998.

- Zakowski, Connie. *Insects on Display: A Guide to Mounting and Displaying Insects.* Highland City, FL: Rainbow Books, 2000.

  Easy instructions on how to best preserve and show insects from beetles to butterflies in a professional manner.

Fly-Tying

- www.fedflyfishers.org/

  Home site of the Federation of Fly Fishers with links to sites that include instructions for fly-tying.

Chapter 8: Insect Gardens
Mystery of Monarch Migration

- www.MonarchWatch.org

  A premier site for monarch enthusiasts, it features everything from butterfly garden tips to the latest monarch research results.

Plan Your Garden

- Henderson, Carrol L. *Landscaping for Wildlife.* St. Paul, MN: Minnesota's Bookstore, 1987.

  A useful guide filled with photographs, garden plans, and tables rating the wildlife value of plants, shrubs, annual and perennial plants.

Insect Calendar

- www.naba.org/sightings/sighting.html

  Part of the North American Butterfly Association's Web site, the daily sightings list includes observations from butterfly enthusiasts across the continent and throughout the year.

- www.learner.org/jnorth

  The home of Journey North, an international phenological collection site where students can record their wildlife observations and track those made by other students.

Insect Repellants

- Henderson, Carrol L. *Woodworking for Wildlife: Homes for Birds and Mammals.* St. Paul, MN: State of Minnesota, Department of Natural Resources, 1992.

  A guide to the habitats, feeding preferences, and nest box construction for North American birds and bats.

- http://midwest.fws.gov/marktwain/kids/crittercrafts.htm

  Patterns for building bird feeders and nest boxes, and information and plans for building a bat house.

Companion Plantings

- Cunningham, Sally Jean. *A Companion-Planting System for a Beautiful, Chemical-Free Vegetable Garden.* Emmaus, PA: Rodale Press, Inc., 2000.

- www.eapmcgill.ca/Publications/EAP55.htm
  Both sources offer information about companion plants and additional suggestions of companion plant combinations.

Additional Web Sites Worth Visiting

- www.cindyblobaum.com
  For additional insect activities or to chat with the author of *Insectigations!*

- www.ent.iastate.edu
  As the home of the Extension Service in Iowa, Iowa State University's Department of Entomology Web site offers assistance in identifying insects found in the state, with plenty of information about how to control pest species. The site's highlight is the Web cam insect zoo. Visitors take turns running the remote control camera to zoom in on a giant cockroach, tobacco hornworm, or whatever other live insect is on display.

- www.entm.purdue.edu/bugbowl/
  Each April as part of the annual Spring Fest, the Purdue University Entomology Department hosts the Bug Bowl. It features edible insects such as chocolate covered crickets, an insect petting zoo, educational exhibits, craft booths, and wacky contests including cricket spitting and cockroach races. The entomology home page provides access to hundreds of interesting articles providing details about insect lives and habits.

- www/life.uiuc.edu/entomology/egsa/ifff.html
  The Insect Fear Film Festival at University of Illinois has gained international attention by showing films that are entomologically wrong, then explaining the truth behind the scenes. During intermissions, insect snacks are served, and moviegoers have the opportunity to view and touch live and dead insects.

- www.members.aol.com/YESedu/welcome.html
  The home page for the Young Entomologist's Society, the site includes a mini-beast museum, listing of state insects, and some limited information for teachers.

- www.insectclopedia.com
  A thorough database with sections on insect identification, research, control, clubs, museums, and schools.

- www.uky.edu/Agriculture/Entomology/ythfacts/entyouth.htm
  One of the best insect Web sites for kids, the University of Kentucky Department of Entomology features insect crafts projects, recipes, games, book lists, helpful links and information about its annual Night Insect Walk.

Teacher's Guide

Entomology is a study in which the necessary skills can be learned at an early age and used throughout the course of one's life. In truth, it is often the younger students who are the most enthusiastic and adept amateur entomologists, as they have yet to establish an unappreciative attitude toward insects or any preconceived ideas of what to expect. They are eager to learn, full of questions and explanations, and more often than not, willing to get dirty. They love to lift up rocks, sweep nets in grassy meadows, dip into pond water, and set up live traps. Once they have caught their quarry, they handle, poke, prod, and question every last detail. What is it? How do you know? What does it eat? Why does it have big eyes? What are those things on its bottom?

With helping hands and guidance from an experienced educator, students as young as five can complete nearly all the activities in this book. There are several instances where the concepts presented may be more interesting to older students than younger ones. The difference between insect and human muscles, the mechanisms of flight (chapter 2), the properties of sound waves (chapter 5), and water quality testing (chapter 6) are four examples. By using the Web sites and books listed in the resource sections, you can use the activities presented in *Insectigations!* as a springboard to more detailed investigations that will stretch the minds of older students.

While it is unlikely that every student will ultimately become an entomologist, all children benefit from close examination of the natural world and recording their experiences in a journal. Additionally, as is demonstrated in the *Real Entomologist* features, insects can be a part of a career in engineering, robotics, food sciences, and many other fields. The following guidelines should help you locate activities that address topics frequently presented at the listed grade level and that can be performed by each student with minimal instruction or supervision.

Grades K to 1

Raising Mealworms
Leaf Litter Shaker
You're on a Roll!
Butterfly Puddles

Grades 2 to 3

Excellent Exoskeletons
Spontaneous Generation
Colorblind Challenge
Dinner Detour
Buzzing Bug
Insect Amplifier
Insect Trap
Insect Rain
Temporary Terrarium

Grades 4 to 5

Mighty Muscles

Twist-an-Insect

Training Bees

Concentration

Wing Waves

Sweep Net

Fly-Tying a Big Bug

Insectigations! The Game

Science Standards

The premise behind *Insectigations!* is investigation. The information presented supports activities that encourage children to explore and study insects in their environment. While some of the activities have expected outcomes that are explained, many others are open ended, with the results dependent upon the actions and observations of the user. This structure aligns closely with the guidelines presented in the National Science Education Standards, available from the National Academy Press (800-624-6242) or online at www.nas.edu.

Unifying Concepts and Processes

Systems, order, and organization

Evidence, models, and explanation

Change, constancy, and measurement

Evolution and equilibrium

Form and function

Science as Inquiry

Abilities necessary to do scientific inquiry

Understanding about scientific inquiry

Science Standards, Levels K through 4

Life Science Standards

Characteristics of organisms

Life cycles of organisms

Organisms and environments

Science and Technology Standards

Abilities to distinguish between natural objects and objects made by humans

Abilities of technological design

Understanding about science and technology

History and Nature of Science Standards

Science as a human endeavor

Science Standards Levels 5 through 8

Life Science Standards

Structure and function in living systems

Regulation and behavior

Diversity and adaptations of organisms

Science and Technology

Abilities of technological design

Understanding about science and technology

History and Nature of Science

Science as a human endeavor

Nature of science

History of science

Bibliography

Akre, Roger D., Gregory S. Paulson, and E. Paul Catts. *Insects Did It First.* Fairfield, WA: Ye Galleon Press, 1992.

http://allafrica.com. Cocks, Tim. "Desperate Measures" in *Johannesburg Mail & Guardian*, February 17, 2004.

Allison, Linda. *Wild Inside.* Boston, MA: Little Brown & Company, 1988.

Anderson, Margaret. *Children of Summer: Henri Fabre's Insects.* NY: Farrar Straus & Giroux, 1997.

Bailey, Jill. *Bug Dictionary.* London, England: Andromeda Children's Books, 2002.

Berenbaum, May R. *Buzzwords. A Scientist Muses on Sex, Bugs, and Rock 'n' Roll.* Washington, D.C.: Joseph Henry Press, 2000.

Berger, Melvin, and Gilda Berger. *How Do Flies Walk Upside Down?* NY: Scholastic, 1999.

Bingham, Jane. *The Usborne Book of Science Experiments.* London, England: Usborne Publishing, 1991.

Borror, Donald Joyce, et. al. *An Introduction to the Study of Insects.* Philadelphia, PA: Saunders College Publishing, 1981.

Bosak, Susan V. *Science Is—.* Ontario, Canada: Scholastic Canada, 1991.

Clausen, Lucy W. *Insect Fact and Folklore.* NY: The MacMillan Co., 1954.

Forsyth, Adrian. *Exploring the World of Insects.* Ontario, Canada: Camden House, 1992.

Glausiusz, Josie. *Buzz: The Intimate Bond Between Humans and Insects.* San Francisco, CA: Chronicle Books, 2004.

Goff, M. Lee. *A Fly for the Prosecution: How Insect Evidence Helps Solve Crimes.* Cambridge, MA: Harvard University Press, 2000.

Guinness Book of World Records. Enfield, England: Guinness Media, Inc., 1998 through 2004.

Imes, Rick. *The Practical Entomologist.* NY: Simon and Schuster Inc., 1992.

Keith, Tom. *Fly Tying and Fishing for Panfish & Bass.* Portland, OR: Frank Amato Publications, 1989.

Kram, Rodger. "Inexpensive Load Carrying by Rhinoceros Beetles" in *The Journal of Experimental Biology*. Great Britain: The Company of Biologists Limited, 1996.

Krebs, J. R., and N. B. Davies. *An Introduction to Behavioural* [sic] *Ecology.* Sunderland, MA: Sinauer Associates, Inc., 1981.

Lasky, Kathryn. *Monarchs.* NY: Harcourt Brace & Co., 1993.

Leahy, Christopher. *Peterson's First Guide to Insects.* NY: Houghton Mifflin, 1987.

www.lhh.org/noise/decibel.htm (League for the Hard of Hearing Noise Center)

www.monarchwatch.com

Pyle, Robert Michael. *Chasing Monarchs.* NY: Houghton Mifflin Company, 1999.

Robertson, Matthew. *Reader's Digest Pathfinders: Insects and Spiders.* Pleasantville, NY: Reader's Digest Children's Publishing, Inc., 2000.

Ross, Herbert H., Charles A. Ross, and June R. P. Ross. *A Textbook of Entomology.* NY: John Wiley and Sons, 1982.

VanCleave, Janice. *Play and Find Out About Bugs: Easy Experiments for Young Children.* NY: John Wiley and Sons, 1999.

http://www.sws-wis.com/lifecycles/

Waldbauer, Dr. Gilber. *Handy Bug Answer Book.* Detroit, MI: Visible Ink Press, 1998.

http://yucky.kids.discovery.com/noflash/roaches/pg000215.html

Zim, Herbert S., and Clarence Cottam. *Insects: A Golden Guide.* NY: Golden Press, 1987.

Index

Other Books from Chicago Review Press

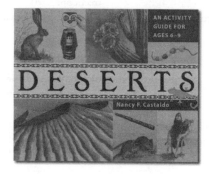

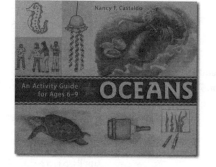

Deserts
An Activity Guide for Ages 6–9
By Nancy F. Castaldo

Introducing children to the wild and often misunderstood environment of the desert and the people and cultures that thrive in and around them. Filled with engaging activities and ideas on how children can help protect these delicate environments.

Illustrated throughout
$14.95 (CAN $22.95) 1-55652-524-9

Oceans
An Activity Guide for Ages 6–9
By Nancy F. Castaldo
*A selection of the Primary Teacher's Book Club

"Using fun activities and games, *Oceans* brilliantly underscores the connection that kids have with the oceans."

—Barbara Jeanne Polo, executive director, American Oceans Campaign

Illustrated throughout
$14.95 (CAN $22.95) 1-55652-443-9

Rainforests
An Activity Guide for Ages 6–9
By Nancy F. Castaldo

Rainforest-inspired activities introduce children to plants, animals, and people that contribute to the beauty of these forests, and encourage young readers to become active defenders of the rainforests no matter where they live.

Illustrated throughout
$14.95 (CAN $22.95) 1-55652-476-5

Available at your favorite bookstore or by calling (800) 888-4741.
www.chicagoreviewpress.com

CHICAGO
REVIEW
PRESS

Distributed by Independent Publishers Group
www.ipgbook.com